Java Coding with Android programming 1

From the performance assessment of middle and high schools
To the applicants preparing for employment

Subtitle : Java Language Beginner 1
  - Development Environment & Variable & Conditional sentence (if else, switch case)

Author : Dennis (Donggeun Jung)

2015.08 Writing Book - Tizen Native Application development guide book
2014.08 Writing Book - Making and understanding Android programming
2013.09 Writing Book - Tizen WebApp Application development guide book
2013.01 Writing Book - Making and understanding WebApp & Hybrid App programming
2011.12 Writing Book - Learning by following bada Mobile application
2009.06 Writing Book - Visual C++ Windows skin & theme programming
1999.11 Begin Computer programmer work
1996.02 Graduate KyungBook University
1995.10 Information Processing Engineer Level 1 Certificate Acquisition

Email : topsan72@gmail.com | topofsan@naver.com

■ Introduction

What is this textbook?

This is a lecture on coding and creating apps and games that can be installed and run on Android phones.
This is a lecture that will be helpful to everyone from performance evaluation of middle school and high school students to job seekers who want to become a professional programmer.
You can study the theory, practice, and development of your apps at the same time and have fun coding.
You can also create your own apps and install them on your phone.

Why should I learn coding?

The purpose of learning coding is to improve the ability to think logically. Making a command to a computer is a lot different from talking to a person. Because the computer can understand only computer programming language.

Do ordinary people who do not care about coding have to learn coding?

Talking to a computer is a lot of patience, but if you have exactly delivered the command, it will be done. People make mistakes, but computers do not make mistakes. The Alpha Go's movement, which looked like a mistake in the match with Lee Sedol in March 2016, was actually a thoroughly calculated strategy.
In this sense, it is helpful for ordinary people to learn coding to live their life.

So how do I study to learn coding?

No matter what kind of discipline, practice is important.
Knowing only coding theory does not help you to grow your logic. Repeatedly doing many exercises will improve your ability to think.

The human brain is similar to muscles. Muscle should continue exercise to develop further. When weighing in a gym, muscles grow, and astronauts who travel on a car have less muscle. Likewise, if you want to develop your brain, you should do a lot of thinking exercises.
That is why theories should be learned at a minimum and lots of practice are better.

If you make many examples in this manual, you can understand what the coding grammar means. You can naturally improve your logic while making various examples.

Is not coding useful in real life just educational?

It is worth studying just to improve the logic, but it would be better if it helps the real life. Currently, the most common tool for coding is scratch. This textbook is a little different. In this tutorial you will develop various Android apps by Java language. You can study coding, create your own apps, and install them on your smartphone. Also, if you want to become a programmer like the author, you can learn the real IT techniques.

Should studying be boring and difficult?

There are a lot of people who think that study hard makes good memory. I do not mean to say wrong, but if I study it, I think learning to have fun makes feel easy and concentration is higher. Maybe you have heard this sentence?
'A genius can not follow a hard worker, and a hard worker can not follow who enjoy he's work.'
This tutorial will help you learn coding and smartphone application development by making simple games and apps.

Why do I have to learn the Java language among various computer languages?

Among many computer languages, the C series takes up 50 percent of the market. C, C++, C#, and Java are C series languages. That's why learning the Java language is like learning C and C++. Scratch or Python is easy to learn, but after learning an easy langue you may feel difficult to learn other languages. The C series language is difficult to learn at first, but after you get used to it, you can easily learn other languages.

I don't know anything about coding. Is it difficult to develop an Android application?

I made this book even beginners can study alone, and develop smartphone apps. As you read and practice making sample apps through the textbook, you will find yourself becoming an expert.

- Aug. 31. 2016   Dennis (Donggeun Jung)   -

Contents

Contents .... - 4 -

- A. Creating an Android development environment .... - 6 -
  - 1) Download JDK(Java Development Kit) .... - 6 -
  - 2) Installing JDK(Java Development Kit) .... - 7 -
  - 3) Download Android Studio setup file .... - 8 -
  - 4) Install Android studio .... - 10 -
- B. Running Sample Project to Emulator .... - 12 -
  - 1) Create a new source project .... - 12 -
  - 2) Run source project to Emulator .... - 17 -
- C. HelloWorld - Change property of TextView .... - 24 -
  - 1) Change TextView widget property .... - 24 -
  - 2) Changing text of TextView widget by Source code .... - 27 -
- D. How to use Variable .... - 32 -
  - 1) Integer variable .... - 32 -
  - 2) Real number variable .... - 35 -
  - 3) String variable .... - 36 -
  - 4) Addition of String variable and Numeric variable .... - 38 -
- E. Arithmetic operator(+,-,*,/,%) - 92% failing question .... - 41 -
  - 1) Type of Arithmetic operator .... - 41 -
  - 2) Complex Arithmetic operate .... - 43 -
  - 3) Problem that 92 percent people can not solve .... - 44 -
- F. Button widget & change String type .... - 47 -
  - 1) Add Button widget in Layout file .... - 47 -
  - 2) Add member variable & event function .... - 49 -
  - 3) Change type of String .... - 51 -
- G. EditText & Simple calculate App .... - 55 -
  - 1) How to use EditText .... - 55 -
  - 2) Input two numeric value and calculate .... - 58 -
- H. BMI (Body Mass Index) calculator .... - 67 -
  - 1) Screen layout configuration .... - 68 -
  - 2) Write the source code .... - 71 -
- I. If - else conditional statement .... - 76 -
  - 1) if statement - in case true .... - 76 -
  - 2) if-else condition statement - in case false .... - 82 -
- J. Get Maximum & Minumun .... - 86 -
  - 1) Getting the Minimum value .... - 86 -
  - 2) Getting the Maximum value .... - 88 -
- K. Create Random number & boolean variable .... - 92 -
  - 1) boolean variable .... - 92 -
  - 2) Random number generation .... - 95 -
  - 3) Create random number by using minimum value .... - 96 -

- L. Even & Odd game .... - 99 -
  - 1) Function of Odd Button .... - 99 -
  - 2) Function of Even Button .... - 101 -
- M. Toast message .... - 105 -
  - 1) Toast message display .... - 105 -
  - 2) Change the position of Toast message .... - 109 -
- N. Multiplication table game .... - 111 -
  - 1) Create multiplication table question .... - 111 -
  - 2) Judging the correct answer .... - 112 -
- O. switch-case conditional statement .... - 117 -
  - 1) Generate Random number .... - 118 -
  - 2) switch case conditional statement .... - 122 -
- P. Number up & down game .... - 125 -
  - 1) Implement 'Result' Button's functionality .... - 125 -
  - 2) Implement 'New game' Button's functionality .... - 127 -
- Q. Rock, Paper, Scissors game & complex operator .... - 130 -
  - 1) Select rock, paper, scissors by Random number .... - 130 -
  - 2) Determine the winner of game .... - 134 -
- R. Installing Application to Smart Phone .... - 142 -
  - 1) Enable smartphone debug mode .... - 142 -
  - 2) Connect PC and smartphone by USB cable .... - 143 -

A. Creating an Android development environment

Before you learn coding, let's create an environment where you can develop an Android app. Because the Android development tools are distributed free of charge, the installation process has to go through several stages. Fortunately, the installation process has been greatly simplified since 2013.
Currently, the following changes have been made. If you install only the Android studio, from the IDE (Integrated Development Environment) to the SDK manager is solved at once.
[Installing JDK 〉 Installing Android Studio 〉 Creating an emulator]

[Key point of this chapter]

```
# The sequence of creating Android development environment #
- Download JDK setup fil
- Install JDK
- Download Android Studio setup file
- Install Android Studio
```

1) Download JDK(Java Development Kit)
Android requires the Java SDK because it uses Java as its development language. Just follow the steps below.

(1) Run Web browser (Chrome, Safari, or Microsoft Edge) and connect to http://www.oracle.com/technetwork/java/javase/downloads.

(2) Click the 'Java DOWNLOAD' button (or JDK DOWNLOAD) and check 'Accept License Agreement' when the screen is changed.

(3) Download the Java SE Development Kit xux. You can select from the various lists the version corresponding to the operating system you are using. If you are using a 32-bit operating system, click 'Window x86'. If you are using a 64-bit operating system, click 'Window x64'.

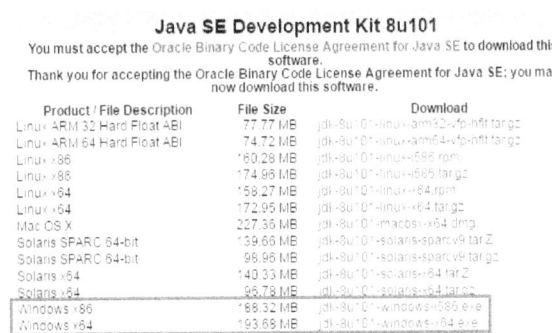

[Tip!] Android Studio only supports Java SDK 1.8 or higher. So you need to install JDK 1.8 or later.

2) Installing JDK(Java Development Kit)

(1) Double-click on the downloaded executable file and the installation screen appears. Click the Next button. When the screen appears, leave the default settings and click the Next button.

 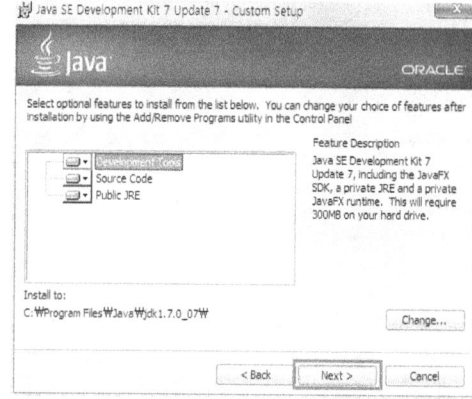

(2) When the JDK installation begins, wait until it finishes. On the 'Java Setup - Destination Folder' screen, click the 'Next' button. If you want to set the installation path to a folder other than the default folder path, click the 'Change' button and change it.

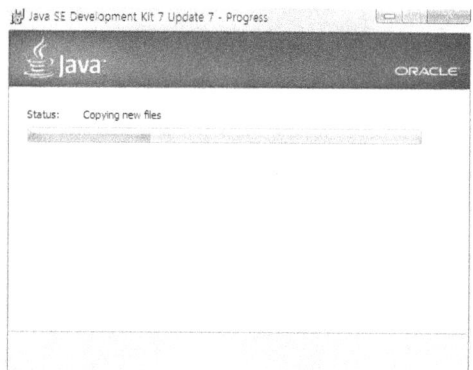 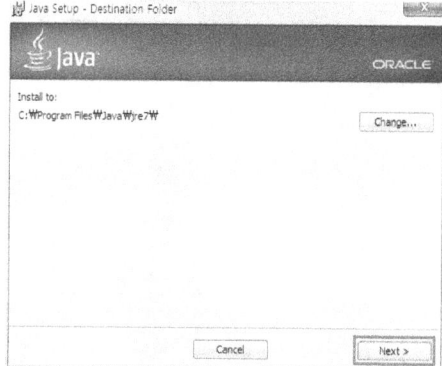

(3) When the JRE installation begins, wait until it finishes. When the installation is finished, click the 'Close' button and finish the installation.

 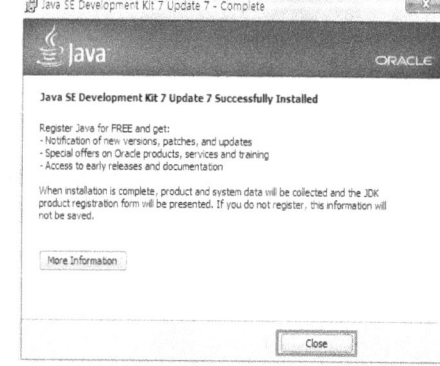

☐) Download Android Studio setup file

If you have finished installing the JDK, let's install the Android studio. Let's create a working folder in advance to save the source project files. Create a new folder at the root of the C: drive, and name it as 'android-work'.

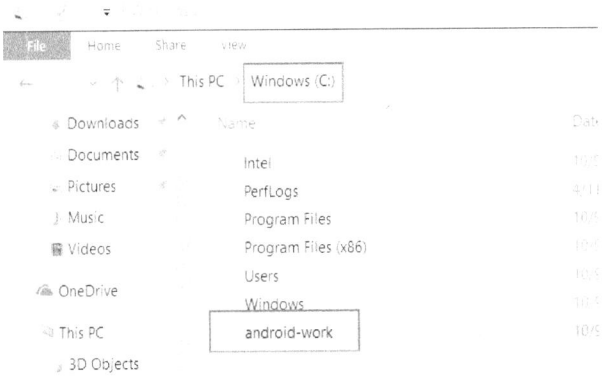

Let's download Android Studio setup file.
- Run web brower(Chrome, Microsoft Edge, or Safari)
- Connect to 'http://developer.android.com/sdk'
- Press 'DOWNLOAD ANDROID STUDIO' button

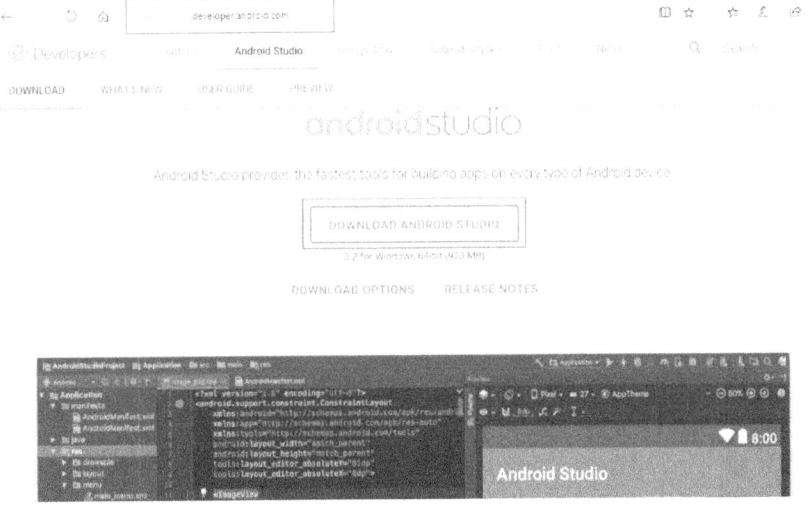

- Check to 'I have read and agree with the above terms and conditions'
- Press 'DOWNLOAD ANDROID STUDIO' button
- Wait until download is finished

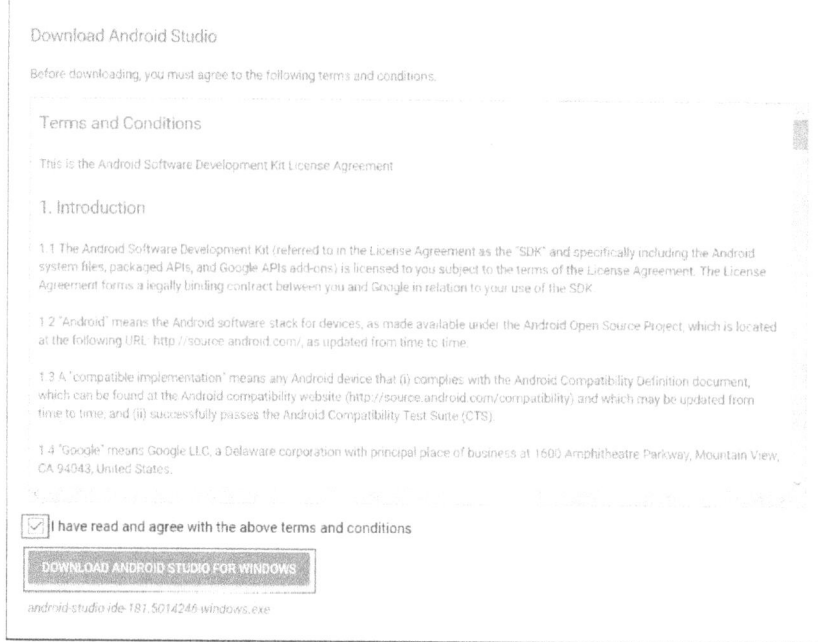

☐) Install Android studio
- After downloading, run the downloaded installation file. Press Next button.
- When the installation selection options screen appears, click the Next button.

 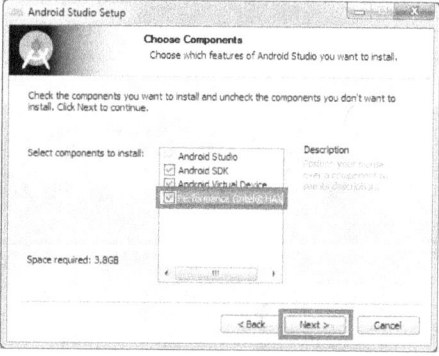

- When the Android SDK License Agreement screen appears, click the I Agree button.
- When the Intel HAXM License Agreement screen appears, click the I Agree button.

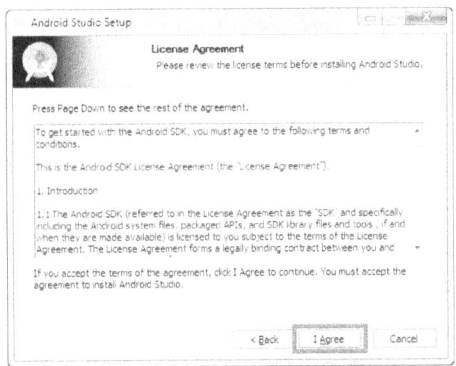 

- When changing the Android Studio installation path and the Android SDK installation path screen appears, specify the appropriate path and click the Next button. You do not need to make any changes.
- When the installation begins, wait for it to complete.

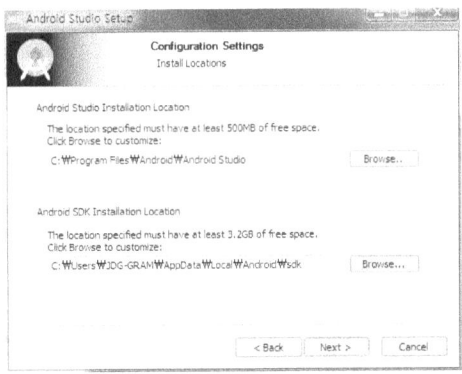 

- When the installation is complete, click the Next button.
- Check 'Start Android Studio' and click the Finish button.

Java Coding with Android programming 1   Dennis (Donggeun Jung)

B.   Running Sample Project to Emulator

[Key point of this chapter]

The sequence of running sample project to emulator #   - Create a new source project   - Create a new emulator in AVD manager   - Run a emulator   - Install a source project to emulator

1) Create a new source project

- When the Android Studio is running for the first time, a screen appears to select whether to load the existing settings. If you are installing for the first time, select 'Do not import settings' and click the OK button.
- On the 'Welcome' screen, click the 'Next' button.

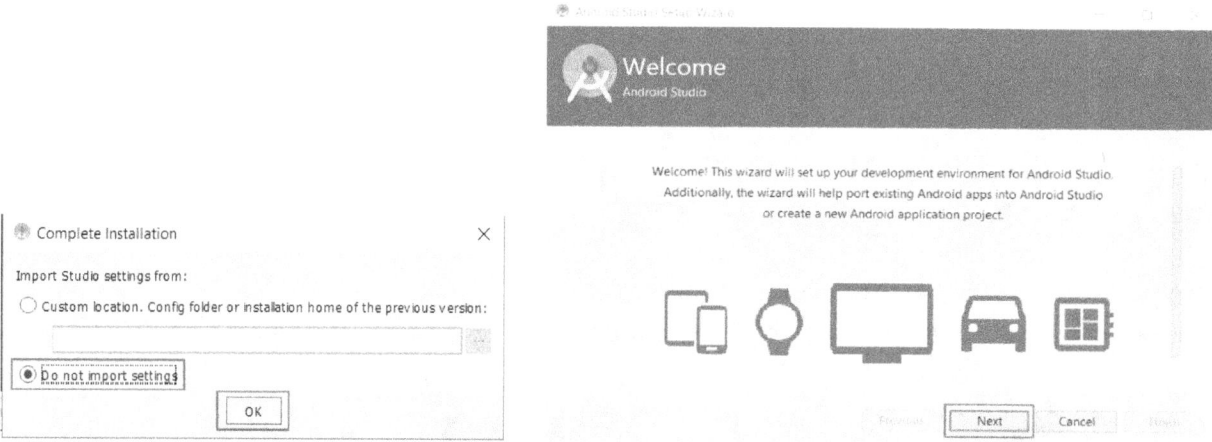

- On the 'Install Type' screen, check Standard option, and click 'Next' button.
- On the 'Select UI Theme' screen, select the desired screen mode and click the 'Next' button. If you have no idea, select 'Intellij'.

Java Coding with Android programming 1 — Dennis (Donggeun Jung)

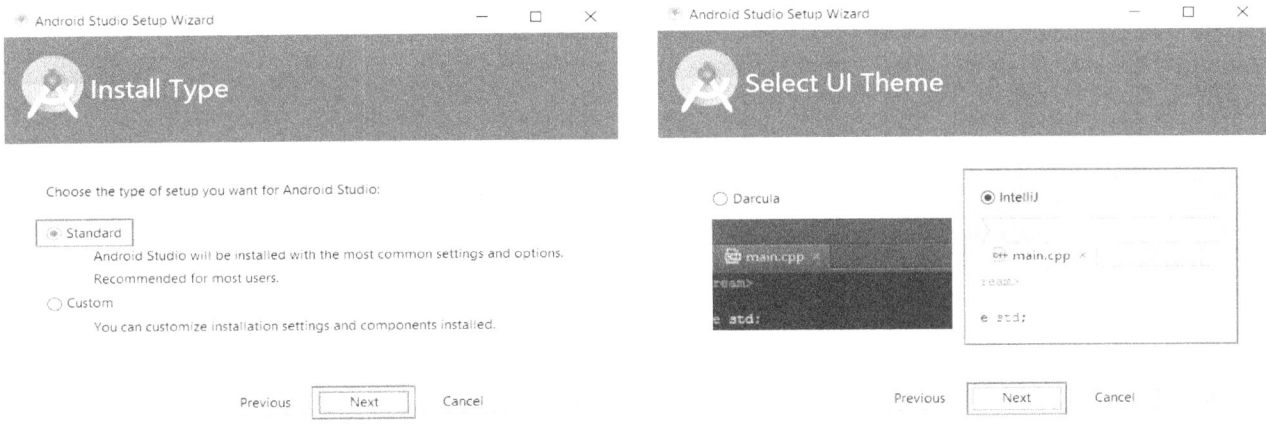

- On the 'SDK Components Setup' screen, you can change the SDK storage folder. Leave the default settings and click the Next button.
- On the 'Verify Settings' screen, click the 'Finish' button to start the SDK installation.

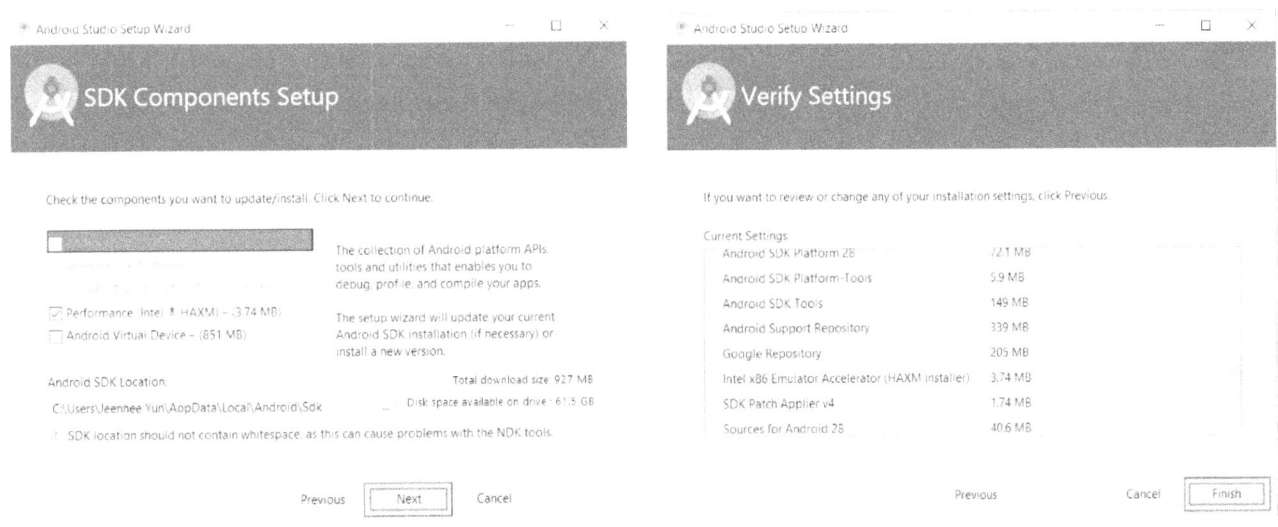

- Wait for the installation to complete. If a pop-up dialog appears, click 'OK'.
- Click 'Finish' after installation is finished.

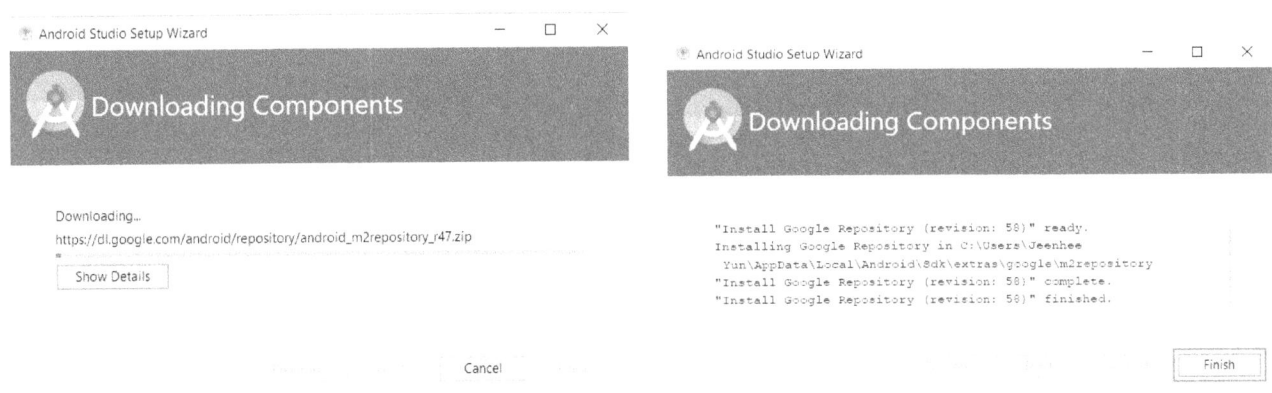

When the Android studio is running, let's create an example. Select 'Start a new Android Studio project'. The project means an application.

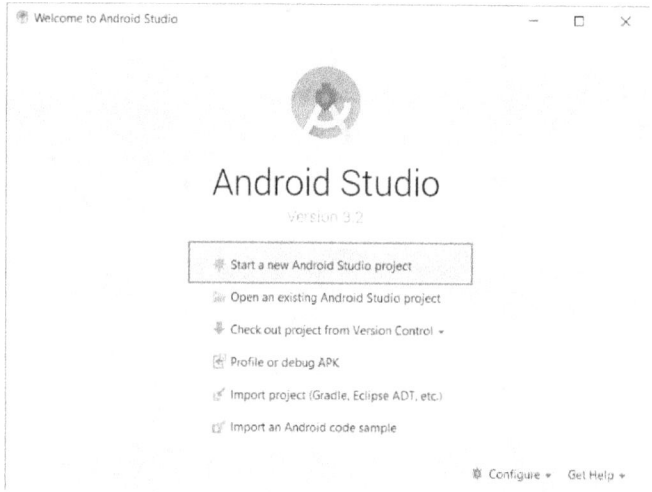

On the 'Create android Project' screen, specify the application name, domain address, and project folder path, and click Next. You can change the project location to C:/android-work you just created.
- Application name : HelloWorld
- Company Domain : example.com (Don't need to change)
- Project location : C:/android-work/helloworld (Don't need to change)

On the 'Target Android Devices' screen, check the device type for 'Phone and Tablet', select 'API21: Android 5.0 (Lollipop)' in the Minimum SDK and click the Next button.

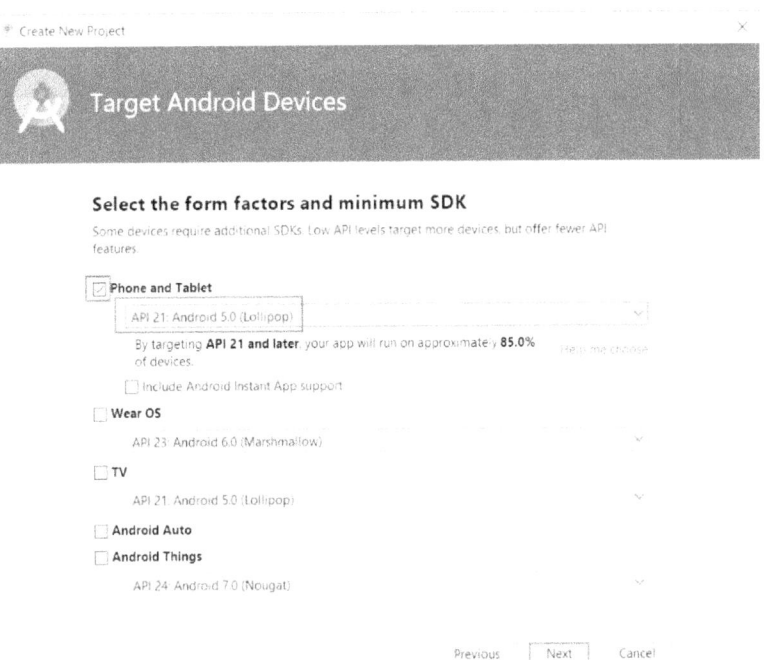

- On the 'Add an Activity to Mobile' screen, select 'Enpty Activity' and click the Next button.
- On the 'Configure Activity' screen, leave the default settings and click the Next button.

On the Component Installer screen, wait for the installation to finish and click the Finish button.

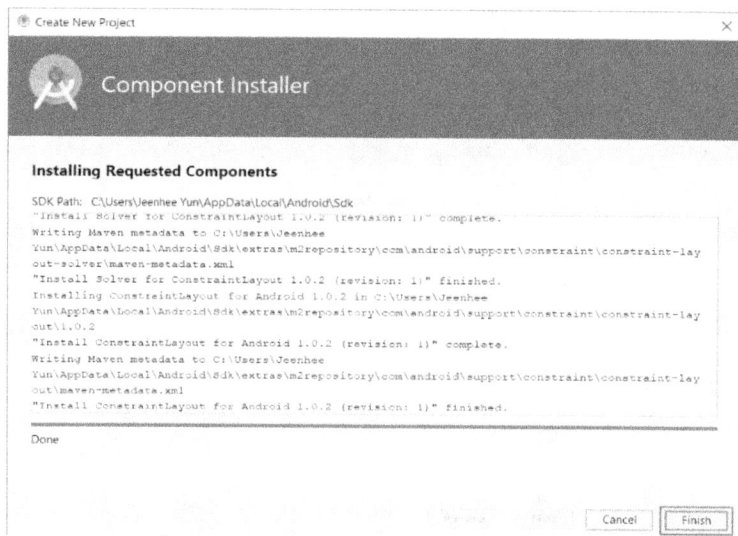

Wait a few moments and the IDE (Integrated Development Environment) will launch and a new source project will be created. If 'Failed to find Build Tools ~' is appear at the bottom of the screen, click the blue letter.

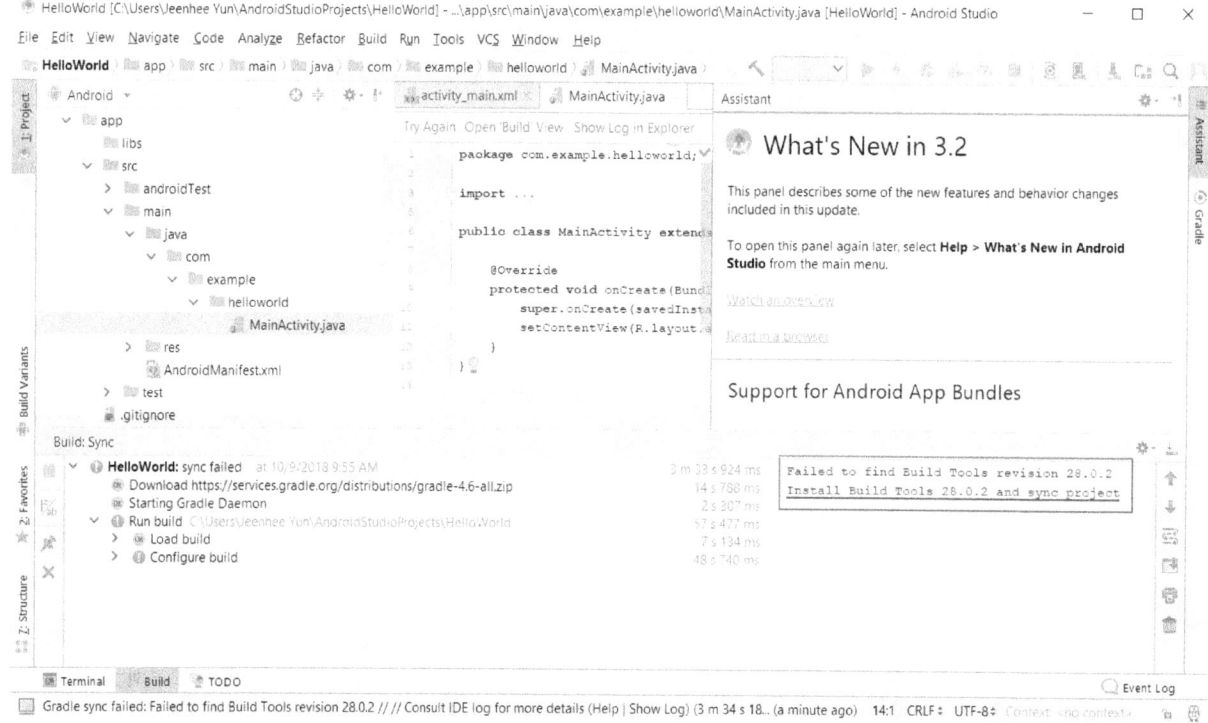

- On the 'License Agreement' screen, check Accept and click the Next button.
- When the installation is complete, click the Finish button.

Java Coding with Android programming 1   Dennis (Donggeun Jung)

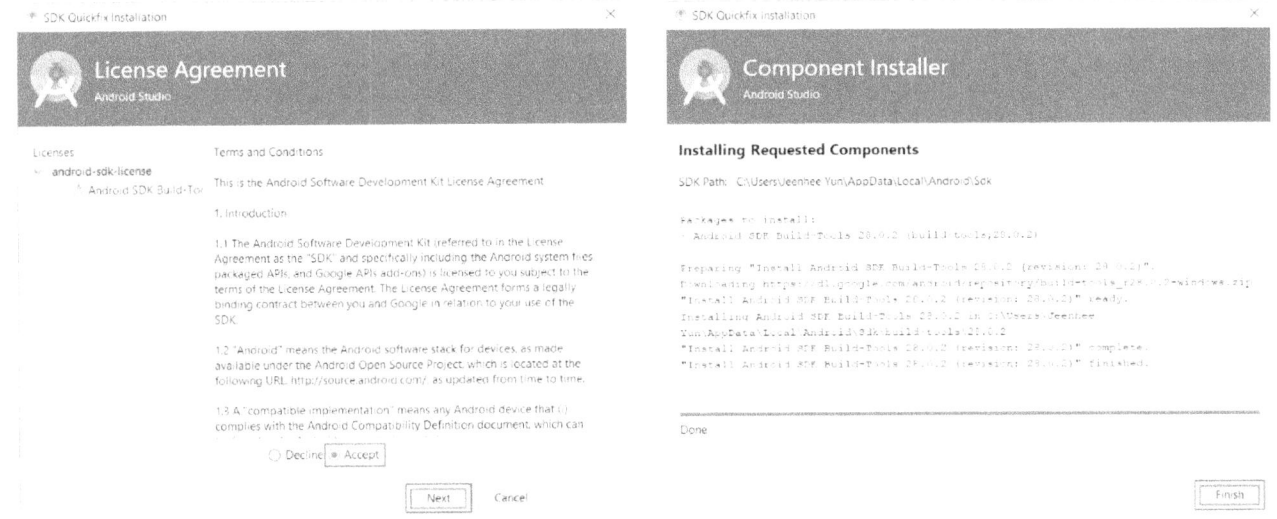

2) Run source project to Emulator

Let's run the example by using the emulator. Android Studio automatically compiles Java code. When an application developer modifies the code, the executable file is built immediately. So you do not have to build it by hand.

You have to run the AVD Manager to run an emulator. The Android emulator is called Android Virtual Device (AVD), and you can create and run an emulator in the AVD Manager.
- Click the main menu [Tools 〉 AVD Manager].
- On the 'Your Virtual Devices' screen Click 'Create Virtual Device' button.

On the Select Hardware screen, select [Category 〉 Phone], select 'Nexus S' in the list, and click Next button.

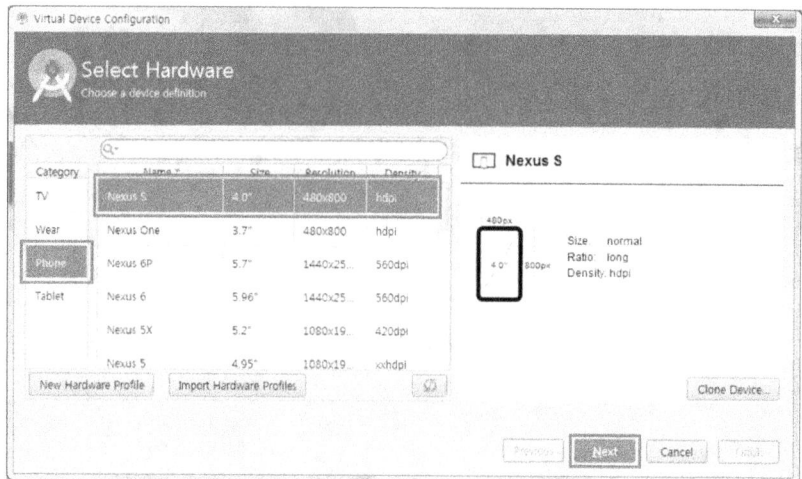

On the 'System Image' screen, click the 'x86 Images' tab button. Select 'Lollipop Download' from the list. If the PC operating system is 32-bit then select [Lollipop Download | x86 | Android 5.0]. If the PC operating system is 64-bit then select [Lollipop Download | x86_64 | Android 5.0].

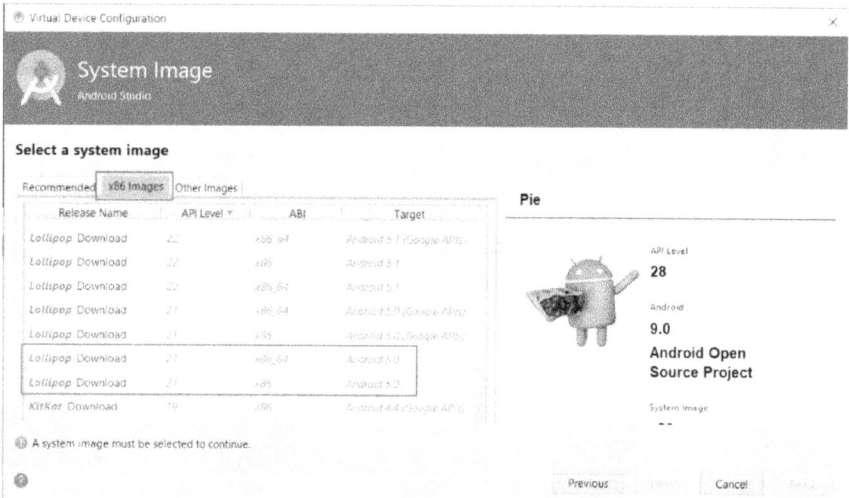

Wait until the emulator image is downloaded. Click Finish when done.

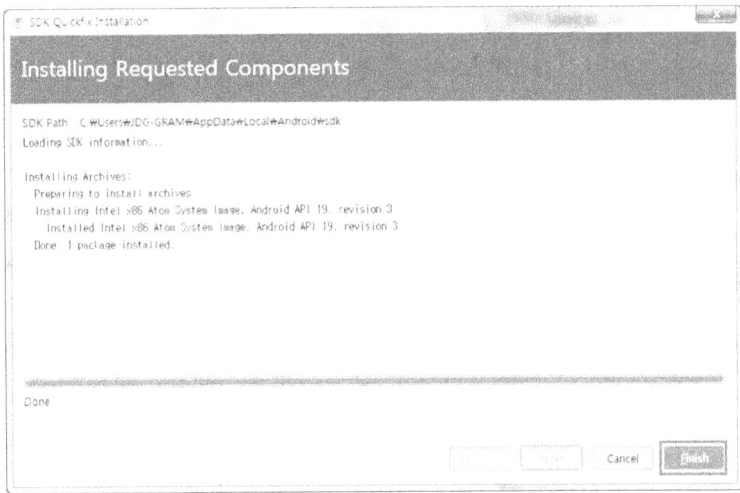

When the 'System Image' screen appears again, select [Lollipop | x86 (_64) | Android 5.0] and click the Next button.

On the Android Virtual Device (AVD) screen, click the Finish button.

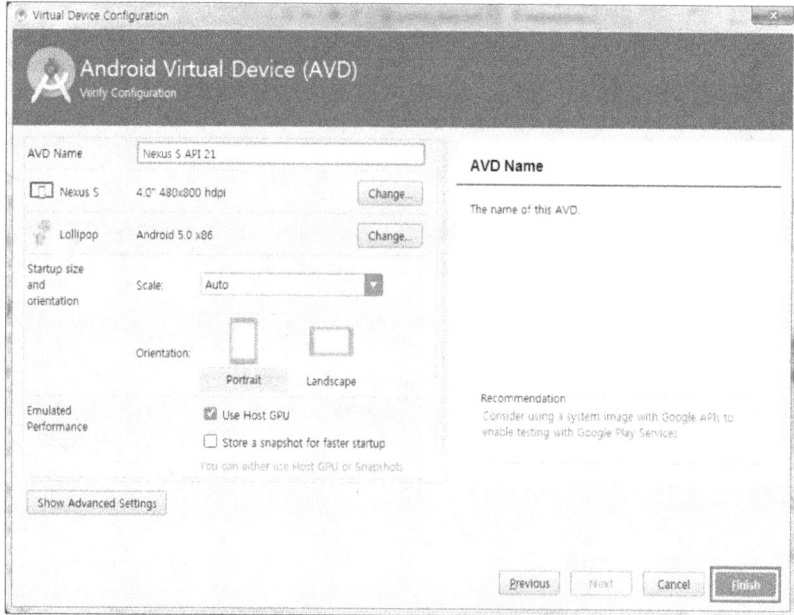

A new emulator was created. If an error occurs, you can reboot. Click the arrow button to the right. The emulator is running. Please wait a moment, until running is finished.

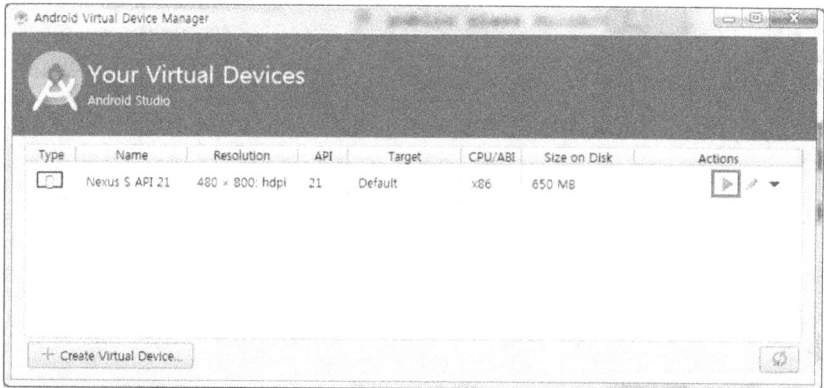

- When the emulator is launched for the first time, the OK button appears. Click the OK button, then it will be disappear.
- Click the icon list button at the bottom of the screen, then click the OK button again.

When the icon lists appear, we will change the monitor off time. Select the Settings icon, and select Display from the list.

Then select the Sleep item and set the monitor off wait time to the maximum. Then press the Back button twice to exit Settings.

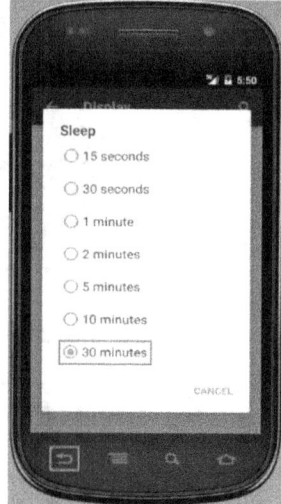

- You are now ready to run the example on the emulator. Selecting the main menu in the Android studio [Run⟩ Run ...] or clicking the Run button on the Toolbar will have the same result.
- If a small pop-up window appears, select the app from the lists.

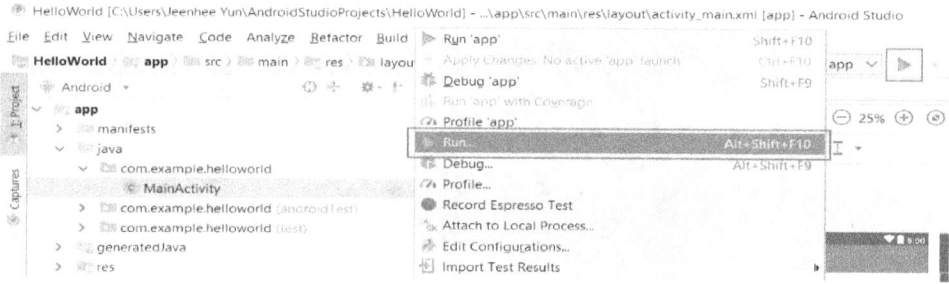

When the pop-up window appears, select the emulator and check 'Use same device for future launches' and click OK.

When the 'Instant Run' popup window appears, click the 'Install and Continue' button.

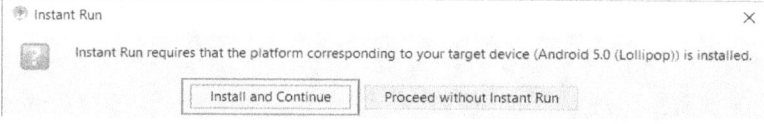

- Click 'Finish' after installation.
- Wait a few moments and the screen of emulator will change and 'Hello World!' is appear. If you see the letter, you have successfully run the example.

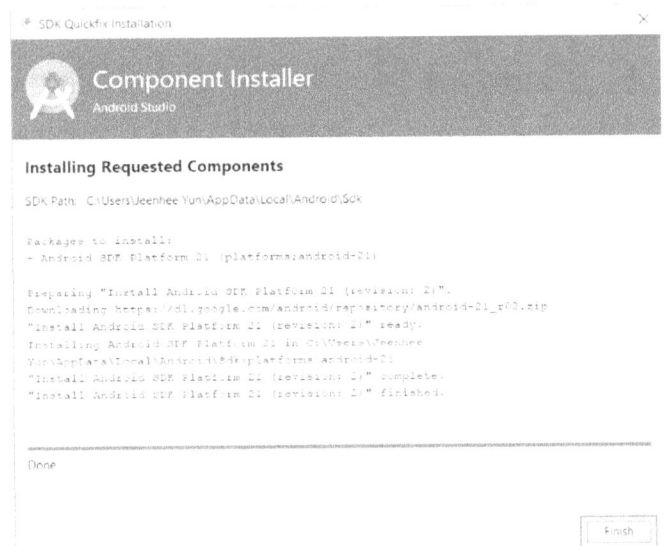

C. HelloWorld - Change property of TextView

[Key point of this chapter]

Change the property of TextView in layout file
- Change the caption text of TextView in Properties list
Ex) Text : This is TextView

Change the property of TextView in source file
- Get the object of TextView : TextView <variable name>= (TextView)findViewById(R.id.<TextView ID>);
Ex) TextView textView1 = (TextView)findViewById(R.id.textView1);
- Change the caption text of TextView : <variable name of TextView>.setText(<String of caption text >);
   Ex) textView1.setText("Nice to meet you");

1) Change TextView widget property

The blue horizontal bar at the top of the emulator monitor is called the title bar or action bar. There is a wide screen below it. In Android, a screen is called Activity.
You can see the word 'Hello World!' on the screen. This is a string representation of a widget called TextView. In Android, controls such as Button, Edit, and Checkbox are called widgets.

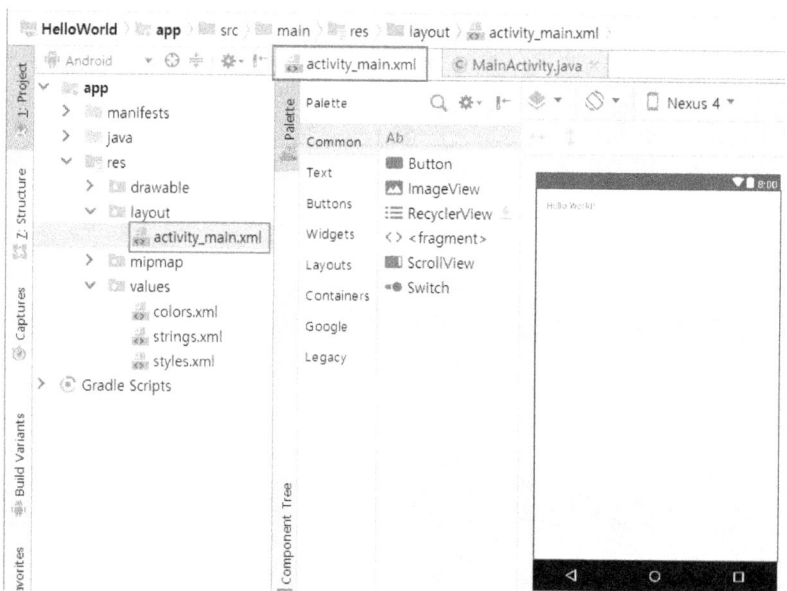

Let's see how to change the string 'Hello World!' which is displayed in the TextView widget. To do this, you need to open the layout information file that stores the screen layout information.

When you create a source project, the activity_main.xml file automatically opens. You can select this file. If the file does not open, double-click [app 〉 res 〉 layout 〉 activity_main.xml] in the tree structure on the left side of Android Studio.

When the layout information file is opened, the same screen as the emulator is displayed.
Depending on the version of Android Studio, you may not see the word 'Hello World!' in the layout information file. In this case, double-click [app 〉 res 〉 values 〉 styles.xml] in the tree structure on the left. When the file opens, add 'Base.' to the code below.

[Before] : <style name="AppTheme" parent="Theme.~
[After] : <style name="AppTheme" parent="**Base.**Theme.~

Then, click the menu [File 〉 Save All] to save the file, and go back to the layout information file and then you could see the word 'Hello World!'.

If 'Hello World!' Is in the middle of the screen, it means ConstraintLayout is used as main layout. A similar layout is RelativeLayout, which we will change for beginners because it is easier.
Press the 'Text' tab button at the bottom-left of the screen and go to text editing mode. And change the word 'android.support.constraint.ConstraintLayout' to 'RelativeLayout'.

[Before] : <android.support.constraint.ConstraintLayout xmlns:android="~
[After] : <**RelativeLayout** xmlns:android="~

When you click the Design tab button at the bottom-left of the screen and go back to design edit mode, the word 'Hello World!' has moved to the upper-left of the screen. Drag the mouse to move the character to the desired position. The TextView widget is moving.

Now let's change the string 'Hello World!' to 'Nice to meet you'. When you click on the word 'Hello World!' a selection mark appears. The TextView widget is selected.
You will see the properties (or Attributes) list in the right side. Here you can change the properties of the selected widget. Scroll down the right vertical scroll to find the 'text' item. The content should say "Hello World!"
Let's delete the contents of the 'text' item and enter the string ' Nice to meet you' by using keyboard. It does not matter if you enter other string you want.

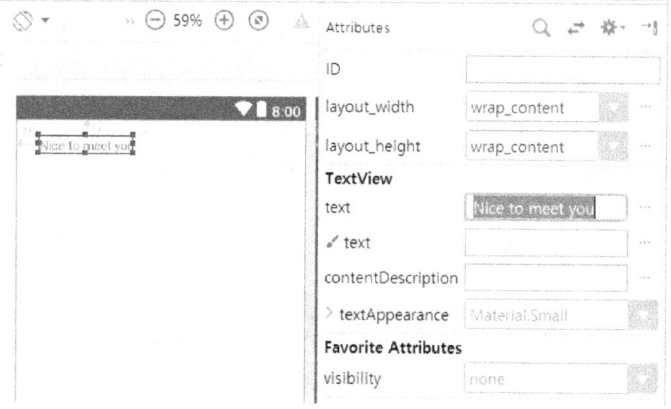

Now let's see what has changed with the emulator. You must save before running. Select [File〉 Save All] from the main menu. Alternatively, you can press the keyboard shortcut Ctrl + S.

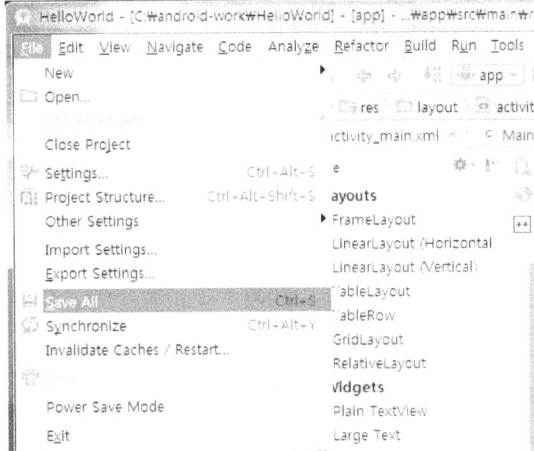

Press the green Run button on the toolbar. Alternatively, you can press the keyboard shortcut Shift + F10. The example now runs on the emulator.
When you run the example again, the string in the TextView widget has changed.

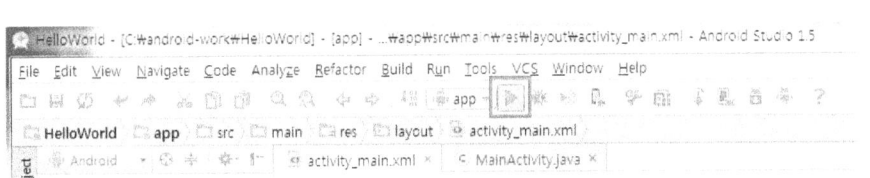 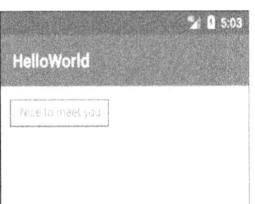

2) Changing text of TextView widget by Source code
We changed the properties of the TextView widget in the layout information file. This method is only available at the first time the app is launched, and can not be changed after launched. So we need a way to change the properties of the widget from coding in the source file.

(1) Default source code
To change the properties of a widget by coding, you must specify an ID for the widget. ID is an attribute that corresponds to a name. Let's look for an ID in the properties list of the layout information file. Type 'textView1' for the content. The ID of the TextView widget is specified as textView1.

[Tip!] The ID of widget can contain English alphabet and number. Other languages and special characters are not allowed.

Now let's open the source file. When the source project is created, IDE automatically opens MainActivity.java, the source file of the main screen. If this file is not opened, double-click [app > java > com.example.helloworld > MainActivity] in the tree structure on the left.

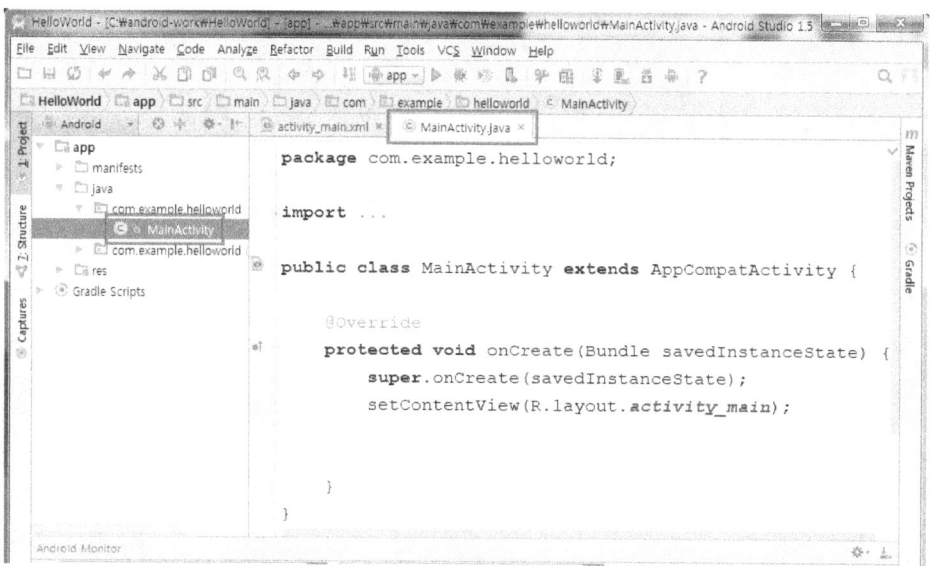

I will briefly explain the code that is automatically generated by default. If you do not understand, just read it once. You would understand what I mean by practicing while making various examples.
The code below refers to the package name of this application. Generally, it serves as an ID for identifying apps. Source files that have the same package name can exchange data with each other freely.

```
package com.example.helloworld;
```

The code below declares the required library.

```
Import . . .
```

Click the '+' symbol on the left side of the above code, and then the details will appear as shown below. It could be different. There are some differences depending on the version of Android SDK. So far, you do not need to modify this code.

```
import android.support.v7.app.AppCompatActivity;
import android.os.Bundle;
```

The code below shows the beginning of a class called MainActivity. An app is made up of multiple classes, and a class is created by combining multiple functions and variables. MainActivity is a class that specifies how the main screen behaves.
'extends' keyword means that it copied another class and created a new class. This is called inheritance. The class on the right is called the base class (or super class), and the class on the left is called the derived class (sub

class). In this case, we inherited a class called AppCompatActivity and created a new class called MainActivity. The contents of the class are enclosed in parentheses '{ }'. So you can add variables and functions between '{' and '}'.

```
public class MainActivity extends AppCompatActivity {
```

The following code shows the header part of onCreate () function. A function is a group of several commands. This is convenient because you only have to call one function when you need to do complicate operations.
onCreate () is a function that runs automatically when an app is running. Specifically, this function is executed when an activity's screen is created. A function that runs automatically when a condition is satisfied in this way is called an event function.
'@Override' means to re-define the function in the base class. It is generally called redefinition.
The contents of the function are enclosed in parentheses '{}'. So you can add commands between '{' and '}'.

```
@Override
protected void onCreate(Bundle savedInstanceState) {
```

The following code shows that it runs the same function in the base class. When you override a function in a base class, it is a good idea to run the original function in this way.
'super' keyword means base class. So super.onCreate () is to execute a function named onCreate () in the base class.

```
super.onCreate(savedInstanceState);
```

The code below specifies a layout information file that corresponds to the face of the activity.
setContentView () is a function that specifies the View that corresponding to the layout. This function should pass one piece of information. The information passed to the function is called parameter. In this case R.layout.activity_main is the parameter.
In R.layout.activity_main, R means the manager that manages the resources used by an app such as layout information, images, and audio files.
R.layout refers to layout files among resources.
activity_main is the file name of the layout file. It is pointing to the activyt_main.xml file, that we have just modified. This way, the same screen as the layout information file will be shown in the emulator.

```
setContentView(R.layout.activity_main);
```

(2) Change text of TextView by Source code
Now we are going to change the text of TextView widget. Add below code at the end of onCreate() function.

[Source code copy link : https://goo.gl/jKooo9 => Code-1]

```
TextView textView1 = (TextView)findViewById(R.id.textView1);
textView1.setText("Welcome! Starting coding");
```

If you take a lot of time typing the source code, you can copy it. Just follow the steps below.
- Launch your web browser and enter the above link address (https://goo.gl/jKooo9). Then the Copy source code page appears.
- Click the button labeled 'Copy Code-1' on the web page.
- Then return to the Android studio, and click on the place where you want to enter the code.
- Press the shortcut key Ctrl + V.

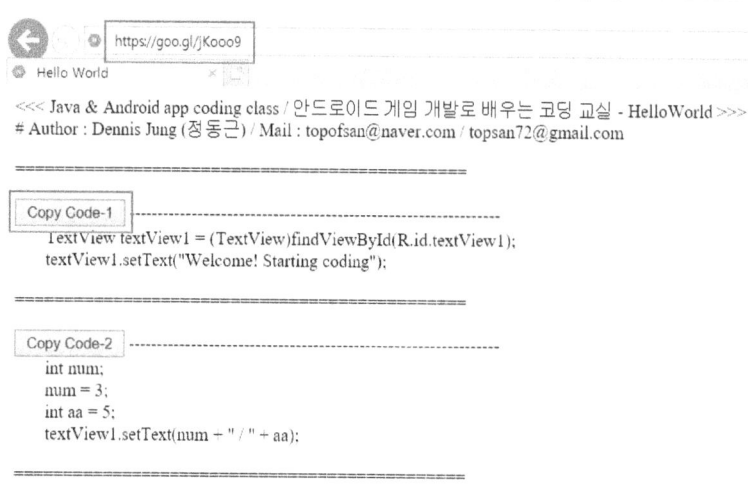

If the balloon appears as shown below, press the shortcut key Alt + Enter. This means that you need to add a library to use a class called TextView. Press Alt + ENTER to automatically add the necessary libraries.

```
public class MainActivity extends AppCompatActivity {
    @Override
    protected void onCreate(Bundle savedInstanceState) {
        super.onCreate(savedInstanceState);
        setContentView(R.layout.activity_main);

        TextView textView1 = (TextView)findViewById(R.id.textView1);
        textView1.setText("Welcome! Starting coding");
    }
}
```

I will explain the newly added code.
The following code creates a variable of type TextView and names it textView1.
findViewById () is a function that finds and returns a widget by ID from a layout file. You must pass the ID of the widget as a function parameter.
R.id.textView1 refers to the ID named textView1.
In front of the findViewById () function (TextView) means to convert the type. The type returned by the findViewById () function is View class, which is the top-level base class for all widgets. So we need to convert it to TextView format.

```
TextView textView1 = (TextView)findViewById(R.id.textView1);
```

The code below changes the text string in the TextView.
textView1.setText (~) means to execute a function named setText () from the contents contained in variable named textView1. You can pass the string to this function as a parameter.
"Welcome! Starting coding" is the string to be changed in the TextView widget, and in the source code the string should be enclosed in double quotes (" ").

```
textView1.setText("Welcome! Starting coding");
```

Let's check the results with the emulator. Save the source file and run it again. The text in the TextView widget has been changed to the string which passed to the setText () function.

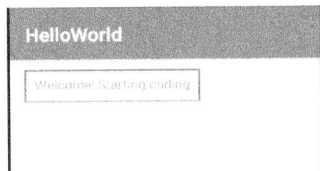

So far, you have seen how to change the properties of a widget with source code.

[Exercise] Create Source Project & Change property of TextView

1. Make new Source Project and set name to 'HelloCoding'.

2. Open Activity's layout file(activity_main.xml).
Change caption text of TextView to 'What is Coding?'.

3. Save source file and run source project to emulator.

4. Open activity source file(MainActivity.java).
And change caption text of TextView to 'To the logical genius'.

D. How to use Variable

Let's start coding study in earnest. The formula below is a problem that can not be achieved by 92%. What is the answer of this question?
7 + 7 / 7 + 7 * 7 - 7 = ?

Where the '/' symbol means division(÷), and * means multiplication(×). Use these symbols for division and multiplication when operating the computer. There is also % sign, which means the remainder value after division. For example, the division value of 7 ÷ 3 is 2, and remainder value is 1. So, 7 % 3 = 1.

So what is the correct answer to the above formula?
56? No. Then what is the real answer? You can ask your computer. To do that, you need to be able to use variables and operators.
The most basic coding grammar is the storage and reference of data. The storage which data can be stored is called a variable. Let's look at the types of variables and how to use them.

[Key point of this chapter]

```
# Type of variables #
- Definition of an integer variable : int <variable name>;
Ex) int num;
- Initialization of and integer variable : <variable name> = <integer>;
Ex) num = 3;
- Definition & initialization of an real number variable : double <variable name> = <real number>
Ex) double num = 10.1;
- Definition & initialization of string variable : String <variable name> = <string>;
Ex) String num = "abc";
- Addition of string variable and numeric variable
String num = "50", sum;
Int aa = 7;
sum = num + aa;     // sum : "507"
```

1) Integer variable

Let's see how to use integer variables by adding new code. Before we do that, we need delete the unnecessary parts of the code that we added before.
Change the onCreate () function as shown below. To delete code you can make block by mouse dragging, and press Del key.

```
protected void onCreate(Bundle savedInstanceState) {
    super.onCreate(savedInstanceState);
```

```
        setContentView(R.layout.activity_main);
        TextView textView1 = (TextView)findViewById(R.id.textView1);


    }
```

Then add the new code at the end of the onCreate () function as shown below.

[Source code copy link : https://goo.gl/jKooo9 => Code-2]

```
    int num;
    num = 3;
    int aa = 5;
    textView1.setText(num + " / " + aa);
```

The complete code for the onCreate () function is below.

```
    protected void onCreate(Bundle savedInstanceState) {
        super.onCreate(savedInstanceState);
        setContentView(R.layout.activity_main);
        TextView textView1 = (TextView)findViewById(R.id.textView1);
        int num;
        num = 3;
        int aa = 5;
        textView1.setText(num + " / " + aa);
    }
```

The following code creates an integer variable named num. int is a variable type that can store an integer. The integer is ... -3, -2, -1, 0, 1, 2, 3, ... The integer includes negative numbers with no decimal point, positive numbers, and zero.
When this code is executed, a 4-bytes space is created in memory, and the name of the memory space is specified as num.

```
    int num;
```

The code below is a code that enters the value 3 into an integer variable called num.
In coding, the '=' symbol does not mean the same, but it means to assign the value on the right to the variable on the left.

```
    num = 3;
```

The code below summarizes two lines in one line.
The first is to create an integer variable in memory and name it aa.
The second is enter a value of 5 to the integer variable aa.

```
int aa = 5;
```

The following code shows two integer variables in the TextView.
If you pass num only to the textView1.setText () function, only 3 is displayed in the TextView.
However, we have combined strings to display both num and aa.
In 'num + "/" + aa' added numbers and letter. This is different with an operation like adding numbers, In this case a number is recognized as a character, resulting in three characters combined into one.

```
textView1.setText(num + " / " + aa);
```

Let's run the example again. The 3 you saved in the variable num and the 5 you saved in the variable aa are displayed in the TextView.

There are several rules for naming variables. You can use English alphabets, numbers. Special characters must be used only with $ and _. Also, the first letter of a variable name can not start with a number.

int is a 4-bytes integer variable type. We are learning about the JAVA language to develop Android applications. The types of basic variable types supported by the Java language are as follows.

- boolean : Express True or False. Ex) true, false
- char : One character. All Unicode characters available. Ex) 'a', 'B', '#'
- byte : 1 Byte integer. Range is -128 ~ 127
- short : 2 Bytes integer. Range is -32768 ~ 32767
- int : 4 Bytes integer. Range is -2147483648 ~ 2147483647
- long : 8 Bytes integer. Range is -9223372036854775808 ~ 9223372036854775807
- float : 4 Bytes real number. Range is $\pm (1.40 \times 10^{-45} \sim 3.40 \times 10^{38})$
- double : 8 Bytes real number. Range is $\pm (4.94 \times 10^{-324} \sim 1.79 \times 10^{308})$

Of these, byte, short, int, and long are all integer variable types. A byte or a short can not store a large number. In general, int type is mainly used. If you need to enter a very large number, you can use long.
float, and double are real variable types. A real number is a number with a decimal point, such as 0.5 or a pi value (3.14). A float can store a sufficiently large number, but if the source code has a real value, it will automatically be recognized as a double. So it is better to use double to make your code more convenient.

2) Real number variable

Let's add a new code to see how to use a real number variable. Before we do that, we need delete the unnecessary parts of the code that we added before.
Change the onCreate () function as shown below. To delete code you can make block by mouse dragging, and press Del key.

```java
protected void onCreate(Bundle savedInstanceState) {
    super.onCreate(savedInstanceState);
    setContentView(R.layout.activity_main);
    TextView textView1 = (TextView)findViewById(R.id.textView1);


}
```

Then add the new code at the end of the onCreate () function as shown below.

[Source code copy link : https://goo.gl/jKooo9 => Code-3]

```java
double num, aa, sum;
num = 10.1;
aa = 1.1;
sum = num + aa;
textView1.setText("sum=" + sum);
```

The complete code for the onCreate () function looks like this:

```java
protected void onCreate(Bundle savedInstanceState) {
    super.onCreate(savedInstanceState);
    setContentView(R.layout.activity_main);
    TextView textView1 = (TextView)findViewById(R.id.textView1);
    double num, aa, sum;
    num = 10.1;
    aa = 1.1;
    sum = num + aa;
    textView1.setText("sum=" + sum);
}
```

The following code creates three real number variables. double is a variable type that can store a real number.

When this code is executed, three 8-bytes spaces are created in the memory, and the names of the memory spaces are specified as num, aa, and sum.

```
double num, aa, sum;
```

Below is the code to enter a real number value of 10.1 in the variable num, and a real value of 1.1 in the variable aa.

```
num = 10.1;
aa = 1.1;
```

Below is the code that adds two real numbers stored in two variables and stores the result in a variable named sum. Numbers can be added together.

```
sum = num + aa;
```

The following code displays the value stored in the variable named sum on the screen. setText () is used to display a string, so it combines letters and numbers into a single string by using '+'.

```
textView1.setText("sum=" + sum);
```

Let's run the example again and check the results. We added 10.1 and 1.1. The result is 11.2.

☐) String variable

Let's see how to use string variable by adding new code. Before we do that, we need delete the unnecessary parts of the code that we added before.

Change the onCreate () function as shown below. To delete code you can make block by mouse dragging, and press Del key.

```
protected void onCreate(Bundle savedInstanceState) {
    super.onCreate(savedInstanceState);
    setContentView(R.layout.activity_main);
    TextView textView1 = (TextView)findViewById(R.id.textView1);


}
```

Then add the new code at the end of the onCreate () function as shown below.

[Source code copy link : https://goo.gl/jKooo9 => Code-4]

```
String num = "abc", aa;
aa = "def";
textView1.setText(num + aa);
```

The complete code for the onCreate () function looks like this.

```
protected void onCreate(Bundle savedInstanceState) {
    super.onCreate(savedInstanceState);
    setContentView(R.layout.activity_main);
    TextView textView1 = (TextView)findViewById(R.id.textView1);
    String num = "abc", aa;
    aa = "def";
    textView1.setText(num + aa);
}
```

Below is the code to create two string variables and enter the string 'abc' in the first variable named num.
The String is a data type class that can store string text. It contains many functions inside the class, so it has many useful functions such as searching, trimming, and replacing.

```
String num = "abc", aa;
```

Below is the code to enter the string 'def' into a string variable named aa.
In the source code, strings must be enclosed in quotation marks ("") before and after.

```
aa = "def";
```

Below is a code that displays the strings stored in num and aa on the screen.
If you put '+' between two strings, they will be combined into one string.

```
textView1.setText(num + aa);
```

Run it again and check the result. 'abc' stored in variable num and 'def' stored in variable aa are combined and displayed as a single string.

Java Coding with Android programming 1 — Dennis (Donggeun Jung)

☐) Addition of String variable and Numeric variable

We tried to add numbers together, and we added letters. So what if we add letter and number? Let's look at an example.

Change the onCreate () function as shown below. To delete code you can make block by mouse dragging, and press Del key.

```java
protected void onCreate(Bundle savedInstanceState) {
    super.onCreate(savedInstanceState);
    setContentView(R.layout.activity_main);
    TextView textView1 = (TextView)findViewById(R.id.textView1);

}
```

Then add the new code at the end of the onCreate () function as shown below.

[Source code copy link : https://goo.gl/jKooo9 => Code-5]

```java
String num = "50", sum;
int aa = 7;
sum = num + aa;
textView1.setText(sum);
```

The complete code for the onCreate () function looks like this

```java
protected void onCreate(Bundle savedInstanceState) {
    super.onCreate(savedInstanceState);
    setContentView(R.layout.activity_main);
    TextView textView1 = (TextView)findViewById(R.id.textView1);
    String num = "50", sum;
    int aa = 7;
    sum = num + aa;
    textView1.setText(sum);
}
```

Below is the code to declare two string variables, and we enter '50' in the first variable num. Because it is a string variable, 50 is stored as a character, not a numeric value. So we can not do addition calculations in this state. The next line declares an integer variable named aa and we entered 7.

```
String num = "50", sum;
int aa = 7;
```

The following is the code that adds the string (50) stored in a String variable and the number (7) stored in an int variable, and displays the result on the screen.

```
sum = num + aa;
textView1.setText(sum);
```

Let's run the example again. We added 50 and 7, but the result is 507 instead of 57. You can not perform addition calculations in string state. 7 stored in the aa variable is changed to a string, and then it is appended to the end of string num.

We have briefly reviewed the basic variable types and how to use them.

[Tip!] String is different from basic variable types like int, double, and boolean.
For example, in case int num = 3; , num is the name of the memory space where the data is stored, and 3 is stored in memory space called num.
But in case String aa = "def"; , String is a class. Computer make storage in memory for String object, and aa has a value that the address of the storage space. A class that is created in memory is called an object or an instance. Actually aa is a numeric variable internally, and if you go to a memory address that corresponds to the number stored in it, there is a String object.
Even if you do not understand, you dont not have to worry about practicing in the future.

[Exercise] How to use the variable
1. Create an integer variable named byte1, and store 256,
Create an integer variable named byte2, and store 65536,
Let's display the values stored in two variables in the TextView.

2. Create 3 real variable named num1, num2, sum.
Save 123.456 in num1.
Save 654.321 in num2.
Add the values of the two variables, save the result in sum, and display them in the TextView.

3. Create two string variable named girl, boy.
Save "Juliet" to girl,
and save 'Romeo' to boy.

Let's display it in TextView by attaching the 2 variables.

4. Save '3' in a string variable named num1.
Save 0.14 in a real number variable named num2.
Let's display it in TextView by attaching the 2 variables.

E. Arithmetic operator(+,-,*,/,%) – 92% failing question

[Key point of this chapter]

```
# Type of arithmetic operators #
- Addition operator : +
Ex) int add = 1 + 2;        // add : 3
- Subtraction operator : -
Ex) int minus = 5 - 3;      // minus : 2
- Multiplication operator : *
Ex)int multi = 2 * 3;       // multi : 6
- Division operator : /
Ex) int divide = 4 / 2;     // divide : 2
- Getting remainder of division operator : %
Ex) int rest = 7 % 3;       // rest : 1
```

1) Type of Arithmetic operator

Below are five formulas. '=' Is an assignment operator. This means that the result value on the right side of the formula is stored in the variable on the left.

+, -, *, /,% These symbols are arithmetic operators that calculate two numbers. '+' Means addition, '-' means subtraction, '*' means multiplication, '/' means division, and '%' means the remainder value after division. For example, the division value of 7 ÷ 3 is 2, and remainder value is 1. So, 7 % 3 = 1.

```
int add = 1 + 2;      // 3
int minus = 5 - 3;    // 2
int multi = 2 * 3;    // 6
int divide = 4 / 2;   // 2
int rest = 7 % 3;     // 1
```

Let's create an example and practice it. Change the onCreate () function as shown below. To delete code you can make block by mouse dragging, and press Del key.

```java
protected void onCreate(Bundle savedInstanceState) {
    super.onCreate(savedInstanceState);
    setContentView(R.layout.activity_main);
    TextView textView1 = (TextView)findViewById(R.id.textView1);

}
```

Then add the new code at the end of the onCreate () function as shown below.

[Source code copy link : https://goo.gl/jKooo9 => Code-6]

```java
int add = 1 + 2;
int minus = 5 - 3;
int multi = 2 * 3;
int divide = 4 / 2;
int rest = 7 % 3;
textView1.setText("1 + 2 = " + add + "\n5 - 3 = "
  + minus + "\n2 * 3 = " + multi + "\n4 / 2 = " + divide
  + "\n7 % 3 = " + rest);
```

The complete code for the onCreate () function looks like this:

```java
protected void onCreate(Bundle savedInstanceState) {
    super.onCreate(savedInstanceState);
    setContentView(R.layout.activity_main);
    TextView textView1 = (TextView)findViewById(R.id.textView1);
    int add = 1 + 2;
    int minus = 5 - 3;
    int multi = 2 * 3;
    int divide = 4 / 2;
    int rest = 7 % 3;
    textView1.setText("1 + 2 = " + add + "\n5 - 3 = "
      + minus + "\n2 * 3 = " + multi + "\n4 / 2 = " + divide
      + "\n7 % 3 = " + rest);
}
```

We added 1 and 2, saved it in an integer variable named add, subtracted 3 from 5, and saved it in minus. We multiplied 2 and 3, saved in multi, divided 4 and 2 saved in divide. Finally, we saved the remainder of 7 divided by 3 into rest.
Then we used the TextView.setText () function to display the five results on the screen. ' \n' is a line break that goes to the next line.

Let's run the example and check the results. The five operation results are displayed in the TextView.

2) Complex Arithmetic operate

There are two formulars below. What is the result?

int calc1 = 2 + 5 - 3;   // 4
int calc2 = 2 + 3 * 3;   // 11

Each formula has two operators. In this case, the result may depending on which formula is calculated first. The rules for calculating two or more complex formulas are:
- Calculate the left formula first, and calculate the right formula later.
- Multiplication (*), division (/) has higher priority than subtraction (+) and subtraction (-). Therefore, multiplication and division are first calculated.

Let's create an example and check the results directly. Change the onCreate () function as shown below. To delete code you can make block by mouse dragging, and press Del key.

```
protected void onCreate(Bundle savedInstanceState) {
    super.onCreate(savedInstanceState);
    setContentView(R.layout.activity_main);
    TextView textView1 = (TextView)findViewById(R.id.textView1);

}
```

Then add the new code at the end of the onCreate () function as shown below.

[Source code copy link : https://goo.gl/jKooo9 => Code-7]

```
int calc1 = 2 + 5 - 3;
int calc2 = 2 + 3 * 3;
textView1.setText("2 + 5 - 3 = " + calc1
        + "\n2 + 3 * 3 = " + calc2);
```

The complete code for the onCreate () function looks like this:

```
protected void onCreate(Bundle savedInstanceState) {
    super.onCreate(savedInstanceState);
```

```
        setContentView(R.layout.activity_main);
        TextView textView1 = (TextView)findViewById(R.id.textView1);
        int calc1 = 2 + 5 - 3;
        int calc2 = 2 + 3 * 3;
        textView1.setText("2 + 5 - 3 = " + calc1
                + "\n2 + 3 * 3 = " + calc2);
    }
```

The first formula will have a result of 4, regardless of which operator is calculated first.

```
int calc1 = 2 + 5 - 3;
```

In the following formula, if the '+' operation is first calculated, the result is 15, and if the '*' operation is first calculated the result is 11. In this case, 3 * 3 is calculated first, then 2 + 9 is calculated. So the result is 11 because the multiplication has a higher priority than addition.

```
int calc2 = 2 + 3 * 3;
```

Let's run the example and check the results. The results of two formulas are displayed in the TextView.

☐) Problem that 92 percent people can not solve

Below is a problem that can not be achieved by 92% people. We will ask the computer for the correct answer to this question.

7 + 7 / 7 + 7 * 7 - 7 = ?

Change the onCreate () function as shown below. To delete code you can make block by mouse dragging, and press Del key.

```
protected void onCreate(Bundle savedInstanceState) {
    super.onCreate(savedInstanceState);
    setContentView(R.layout.activity_main);
    TextView textView1 = (TextView)findViewById(R.id.textView1);
```

```
}
```

Then add the new code at the end of the onCreate () function as shown below.

[Source code copy link : https://goo.gl/jKooo9 => Code-8]

```
int result = 7 + 7 / 7 + 7 * 7 - 7;
textView1.setText("7 + 7 / 7 + 7 * 7 - 7 = " + result);
```

The complete code for the onCreate () function looks like this:

```
protected void onCreate(Bundle savedInstanceState) {
    super.onCreate(savedInstanceState);
    setContentView(R.layout.activity_main);
    TextView textView1 = (TextView)findViewById(R.id.textView1);
    int result = 7 + 7 / 7 + 7 * 7 - 7;
    textView1.setText("7 + 7 / 7 + 7 * 7 - 7 = " + result);
}
```

We have written the code to obtain the result of the formula below.
7 + 7 / 7 + 7 * 7 - 7
Let's run the example and check the result.

```
HelloWorld

7 + 7 / 7 + 7 * 7 - 7 = 50
```

Since multiplication and division have higher priority than addition and subtraction, the above formula is as foll
ows.
7 + 7 / 7 + 7 * 7 - 7
= 7 + 1 + 49 - 7
And if you calculate this formula, you get 50.

The complete code for this example is shown below. Thank you.

```
package com.example.helloworld;
import android.support.v7.app.AppCompatActivity;
import android.os.Bundle;
import android.widget.TextView;
```

```
public class MainActivity extends AppCompatActivity {

    @Override
    protected void onCreate(Bundle savedInstanceState) {
        super.onCreate(savedInstanceState);
        setContentView(R.layout.activity_main);
        TextView textView1 = (TextView)findViewById(R.id.textView1);
        int result = 7 + 7 / 7 + 7 * 7 - 7;
        textView1.setText("7 + 7 / 7 + 7 * 7 - 7 = " + result);
    }
}
```

[Example] Arithmetic operator (+, −, *, /, %)
1. Find the answer of below formula, by making Android application.
− 9 + (8 − 5) * (6 + 3) / 9 + 4 = ?

F. Button widget & change String type

In this time, let's create an example that displays the number of times the Button is clicked in the TextView. To do that, let's learn Button widget and string type casting.

[Key point of this chapter]

```
# How to use Button widget #
- Set Button event function name to onClick property in layout file
Ex) onClick : onBtnAdd
- Define Button event function in source file
public void onBtnAdd(View v) {            // Header of Button event function
      textView1.setText("Button clicked");   // Content of function
}                             // End of function

# Type case of string #
- Change string to integer type : <integer variable> = Integer.parseInt(<string>);
Ex)int num = Integer.parseInt("21");       // num : 21
- Change integer to string type : <string variable> = Integer.toString(<integer>);
Ex) String strNum = Integer.toString(10);    // strNum : "10"
```

1) Add Button widget in Layout file

When the user decides to execute some code, the easiest way to do this is to use the Button widget. Let's go to the layout file (activy_main.xml) and add a Button widget.

Click [Common 〉 Button] (or Buttons 〉 Button) in the left palette by left button of mouse, and drag it to the activity screen. Then take it down the TextView widget and release the clicked finger.

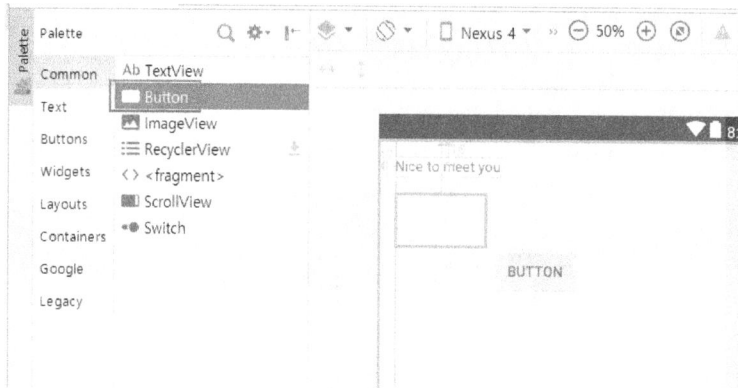

A new Button has been added to the screen. Now specify the caption text for the Button and the event function's name. Find the two items in the Properties list on the right and enter the following informations:
- onClick : onBtnAdd
- text : Add

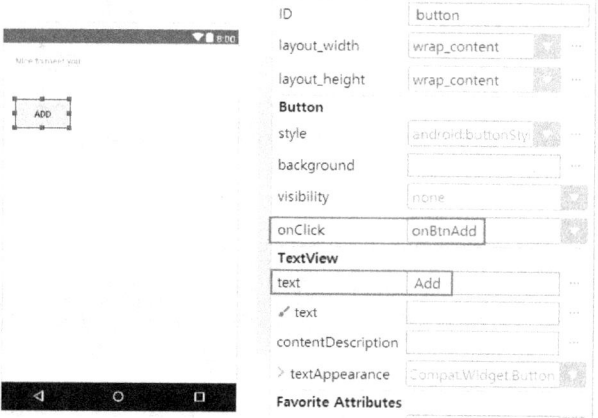

The text property is an attribute that specifies the caption text just like the TextView widget. The onClick property is an attribute that specifies the name of the event function that is automatically executed when the user clicks the Button. This is called the callback function when the app developer specifies the name of the event function. When user click the Add Button, a function named onBtnAdd () is executed.

We will change the text in the TextView to 0. Select TextView and change the text property to 0 in the Properties list.

2) Add member variable & event function

Now you're done with the layout file. Return to the source file (MainActivity.java). And clean up unnecessary code. Change the onCreate () function as shown below. To delete code you can make block by mouse dragging, and press Del key.

```
protected void onCreate(Bundle savedInstanceState) {
    super.onCreate(savedInstanceState);
    setContentView(R.layout.activity_main);


}
```

We also deleted the code that stores the TextView widget in a variable. The reason is that you need to use the TextView variable throughout the class(MainActivity) to change the TextView's text when the Button is clicked. A variable declared inside of function are called 'local variable' and you can not use this variable outside of function. So we will declare the variable outside the function so that it can be used by other functions.
Add the following new code after the beginning of the MainActivity class.

[Source code copy link : https://goo.gl/tHr4tT => Code-1]

```
public class MainActivity extends AppCompatActivity {
    TextView textView1;
```

This allows textView1 to be used by any function, because it is outside of function. A variable outside a function is called a 'member variable', and a variable inside a function is called 'local variable'.

To use this variable to change the properties of a TextView, you must store the TextView object in the variable. This should be done when the app is launched. Add the following new code to the end of onCreate () function.

[Source code copy link : https://goo.gl/tHr4tT => Code-2]

```java
protected void onCreate(Bundle savedInstanceState) {
    super.onCreate(savedInstanceState);
    setContentView(R.layout.activity_main);
    textView1 = (TextView)findViewById(R.id.textView1);
}
```

This code save TextView object in member variable textView1. Because it is a member variable, you can use this variable regardless of any function which is included in same class.

Now, when user presses the Button, computer will display the string 'Add button clicked!' in the TextView. Create a new function under the onCreate () function and name it onBtnAdd (). Let's enter the code below.

[Source code copy link : https://goo.gl/tHr4tT => Code-3]

```java
@Override
protected void onCreate(Bundle savedInstanceState) {
    super.onCreate(savedInstanceState);
    setContentView(R.layout.activity_main);
    textView1 = (TextView)findViewById(R.id.textView1);
}

public void onBtnAdd(View v) {
    textView1.setText("Add button clicked!");
}
```

We have created a new function. A function is a group of various code. If necessary, you can create and use new functions as you wish.
When the user clicks the Button, the following onBtnAdd () function is executed. 'View v' passed as a parameter is the Button object you selected. If multiple functions use one event function, you can use this parameter to determine which Button was selected. If View is displayed in red, press the shortcut key Alt + Enter when a balloon appears.
public void onBtnAdd(View v) {

The complete code for the MainActivity class is as follows

```
public class MainActivity extends AppCompatActivity {
    TextView textView1;

    @Override
    protected void onCreate(Bundle savedInstanceState) {
        super.onCreate(savedInstanceState);
        setContentView(R.layout.activity_main);
        textView1 = (TextView)findViewById(R.id.textView1);
    }

    public void onBtnAdd(View v) {
        textView1.setText("Add button clicked!");
    }
}
```

Let's run the example and check the result. Save the modified file, and run the example in the emulator. Click the Add button to change the text in the TextView.

☐) Change type of String

Let's make a function that displays the count of Button clicked in the TextView. We need two things to do that: First, we need to get the content of the TextView widget. This is done using the getText () function. You can use the setText () function to enter text, or use getText () to get it.

Second, you need to change the string to a number. Since the content of the TextView is string, you have to change the string to a number in order to perform the addition calculation. This is done using the Integer.parseInt () function.

Let's look at a concrete way through an example. First, we will clean the contents of the Button event function onBtnAdd() as follows. To delete code you can make block by mouse dragging, and press Del key.

```
public void onBtnAdd(View v) {
```

}

Then add the new code to the onBtnAdd () function as shown below.

[Source code copy link : https://goo.gl/tHr4tT => Code-4]

```java
public void onBtnAdd(View v) {
    String strNum = textView1.getText().toString();
    int nNum = Integer.parseInt(strNum);
    nNum = nNum + 1;
    strNum = Integer.toString(nNum);
    textView1.setText(strNum);
}
```

Below is the code to get the string of TextView and store it in a String variable named strNum. You can use TextView.getText () to get the string of the TextView widget. However, this function does not pass a String but passes it in CharSequence format. The toString () function changes the CharSequence to a String format.
So you only need to use setText () when entering text in TextView. And you need getText ().ToString () when you want to import text.

```java
String strNum = textView1.getText().toString();
```

Here is the code that changes a String variable to a number. Integer is a class which is a collection of functions related to integer. Integer.parseInt (String) is a function that converts a String to an integer.
This code stores the converted value in an integer variable named nNum.

```java
int nNum = Integer.parseInt(strNum);
```

Below is a code that increase the value stored in nNum by one.

```java
nNum = nNum + 1;
```

The code above is same as below. '+=' means add the value on the right to the variable on the left and save it in the variable again.
nNum += 1;

And this code is same as below. '++' means add 1 to the variable on the left and save it again.
nNum ++;

[Tip!] The C language is a procedural language. The code is executed one after the other in descending order from top to bottom. Procedural language is easy to learn, but because the code is intertwined with each other, it is difficult to copy only the parts that are necessary for use in a new project. In addition, changes will cause a l

ot of bugs in the associated code.
So developers made a new language called C++. C++ means one thing is added to C language. It's object-oriented-programming (OOP), so it's the class. This means that when you modify a part of code, you do not have to touch the other parts of other classes. And it's also easier to reuse the code you've created into new projects. However, there is also a problem with the C++ language. The C++ language contains both procedural and object-oriented grammars, making it a complex language.
So developers gathered the necessary parts and maded a new language. That is JAVA. So JAVA is easy and powerful.

Let's check the results. Run the example again and click the button to increase the number in TextView by 1.

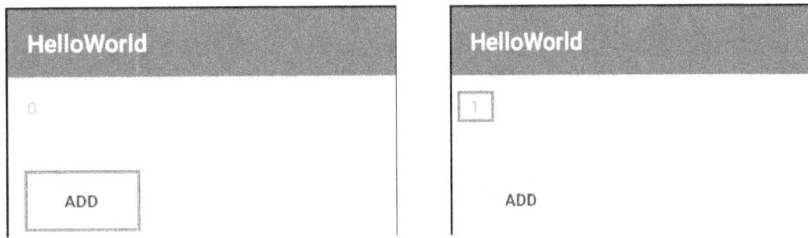

If an error occurs when the button is clicked, go to the layout information file and change the text property of the TextView to 0.

This time we learned how to use the Button widget and String cast. The complete code for this example is shown below. Thank you.

```java
package com.example.helloworld;
import android.support.v7.app.AppCompatActivity;
import android.os.Bundle;
import android.view.View;
import android.widget.TextView;

public class MainActivity extends AppCompatActivity {
    TextView textView1;

    @Override
    protected void onCreate(Bundle savedInstanceState) {
        super.onCreate(savedInstanceState);
        setContentView(R.layout.activity_main);
        textView1 = (TextView)findViewById(R.id.textView1);
    }
```

```java
    public void onBtnAdd(View v) {
        String strNum = textView1.getText().toString();
        int nNum = Integer.parseInt(strNum);
        nNum = nNum + 1;
        strNum = Integer.toString(nNum);
        textView1.setText(strNum);
    }
}
```

[Exercise] Button widget & Change type of String

1. Create a new source project and set name to 'Add2'. Make a TextView and a Button widget in the layout file. Specify the caption text of the TextView as '1' and the caption text of the Button as 'Add-2'.

2. Make a function that increases the caption text of the TextView by 2 each time user click the Button.
1 =⟩ 3 =⟩ 5 =⟩ 7 =⟩ 9 …

G.   EditText & Simple calculate App

This time, let's create an example that the user inputs two numbers and presses one of the four buttons to add, subtract, multiply, and divide. This app display the result on the screen when user presses on of Buttons. We have to use the EditText widget to enter numbers, and add more buttons.

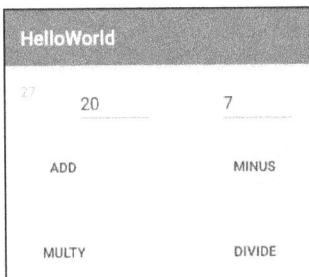

[Key point of this chapter]

```
# How to use EditText #
- Change width of a widget on layout:width property in layout file
Ex) layout:width : 80dp
- Get string entered in EditText by source code : <String variable> = <EditText variable>.getText().toString();
Ex)String strNum = editText1.getText().toString();
```

1) How to use EditText

The EditText widget is the most convenient way for users to enter string. Let's create an example that adds 1 to the number user enter and displays it on the screen. Go to the activity layout file (app / res / layout / activity_main.xml) and add one EditText to the screen.

(1) Adding the EditText widget to the layout file
In the left Palette list, all items in the Text Fields group are EditText widgets. The items are classified according to the purpose of use. When you enter normal text, select Plain Text. Select Plain Text and drag and drop it to the top of the Activity screen, to the right of the TextView.

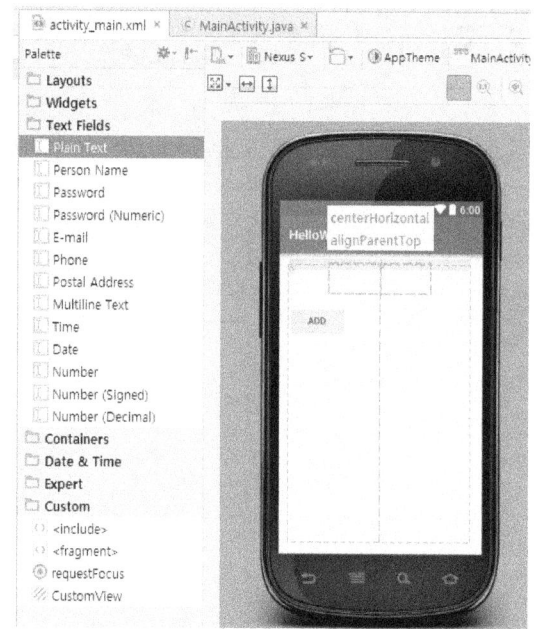
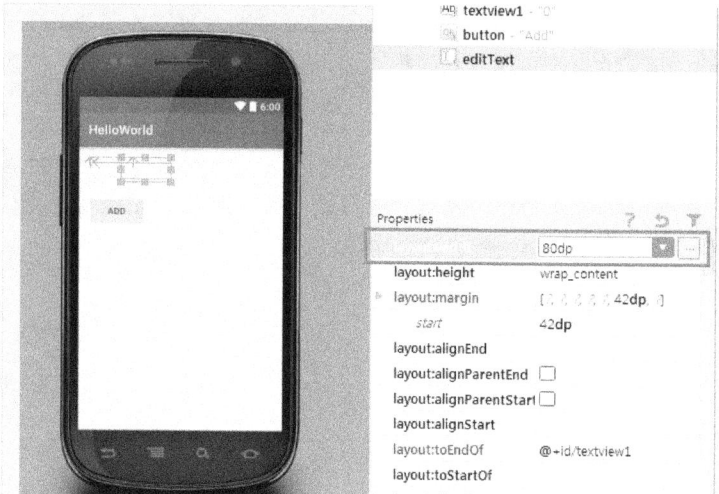

We will change the properties of the newly created EditText widget as shown below.
- layout:width : 80dp
- id : editText1
- text : 0

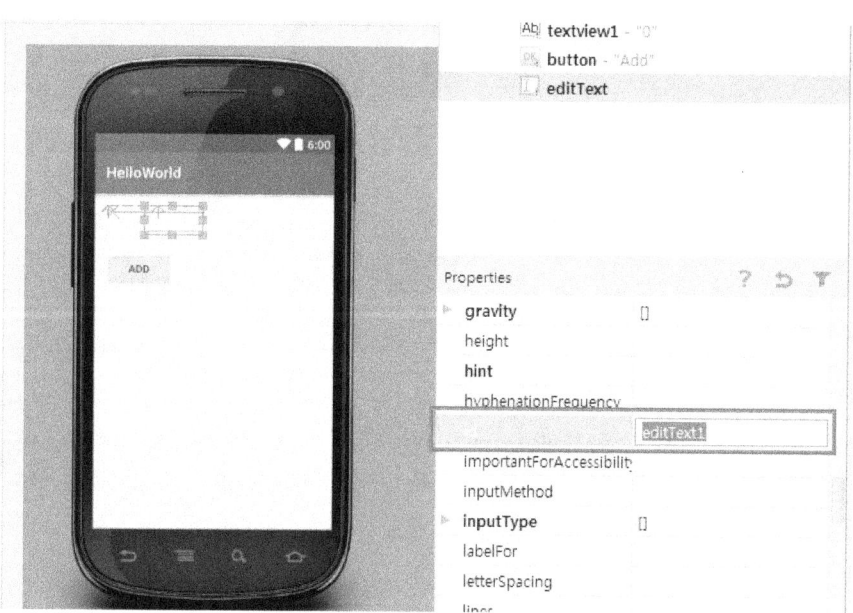

[Tip!] 'dp' is the length unit used by Android and can specify the same logic length regardless of monitor dpi r esolution (density). 1 dp corresponds to 1 pixel when the monitor resolution is 160 dpi (when displaying 160 pi xels per inch). When the monitor resolution is 320 dpi, it corresponds to 2 pixels. So even if the monitor resoluti on is different, the physical size will be the same. The actual length of 146 dp is 146/160 * 1 inch (2.54 cm) = 0. 9125 inch (2.32 cm). The length units used by Android are px (physical pixels), in (inches), mm (millimeters), sp (similar to dp but depending on font settings), em (same text size regardless of font).

(2) Obtaining a string entered in the EditText widget

Let's change the string that the user entered in the EditText widget to a number. We will declare EditText as a member variable so that it can be used anywhere. Go back to the activity source file (MainActivity.java) and add a line of code to the beginning of the class as shown below.

[Source code copy link : https://goo.gl/tHr4tT => Code-5]

```java
public class MainActivity extends AppCompatActivity {
    TextView textView1;
    EditText editText1;
```

When we added a new widget at a layout file, we selected Plain Text in the Text Fields group, but all items in the Text Fields group are equivalent to EditText. So we declare a variable of type EditText as a member variable. When you see a red letter, you can press the shortcut key Alt + Enter.

Save the EditText widget to a newly added variable so you can use it anywhere. Add new code to the end of the onCreate () function.

[Source code copy link : https://goo.gl/tHr4tT => Code-6]

```java
protected void onCreate(Bundle savedInstanceState) {
    super.onCreate(savedInstanceState);
    setContentView(R.layout.activity_main);
    textView1 = (TextView)findViewById(R.id.textView1);
    editText1 = (EditText)findViewById(R.id.editText1);
}
```

When the user clicks the Button, computer has to read the contents of the EditText, changes it to a number, and then adds 1 to it and displays it in the TextView. First, we will clear the contents of Button event function as follows.

```java
public void onBtnAdd(View v) {

}
```

Then enter the required code as shown below.

[Source code copy link : https://goo.gl/tHr4tT => Code-7]

```java
public void onBtnAdd(View v) {
    String strNum = editText1.getText().toString();
    int nNum = Integer.parseInt(strNum);
```

```
    nNum = nNum + 1;
    strNum = Integer.toString(nNum);
    textView1.setText(strNum);
}
```

Below is the code to get the string of EditText and store it in a String variable named strNum. You can use EditText.getText () to get the string for the EditText widget. However, this function does not pass a String but passes it in CharSequence type. The reason using behind the toString () function is to change the CharSequence to a String type.

```
String strNum = editText1.getText().toString();
```

Below is the code that changes the string to a number. Integer is a class which is a collection of functions related to integer. Integer.parseInt (String) is a function that converts a String to an integer type.
This code stores the converted value in an integer variable named nNum.

```
int nNum = Integer.parseInt(strNum);
```

Below is a code that increase the value saved in nNum by one.

```
nNum = nNum + 1;
```

Let's run the example to see the result. When you touch EditText, the keypad appears. Let's enter the number and click the button. A number that is one greater than the number you entered is displayed in the TextView.

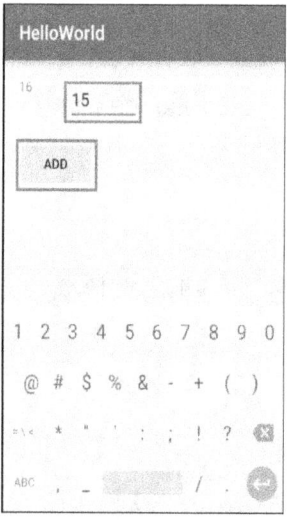

2) Input two numeric value and calculate

Let's create an example where the user enters two numbers and presses one of the four buttons to display the result of the numerical calculation corresponding to that button on the screen. Go to the activity layout file (app / res / layout / activity_main.xml) and add the second EditText to the screen.

(1) Adding a new widget to the layout file
Select Plain Text from the Text Fields group in the left Palette list and drag and drop it to the top - right of the screen to create a new EditText.

We will change the properties of the second EditText widget as shown below.
- layout:width : 80dp
- id : editText2
- text : 0

This example requires four buttons. From the Palette list, open the Common group (or Buttons group) and select the Buton item to add three buttons to the screen.

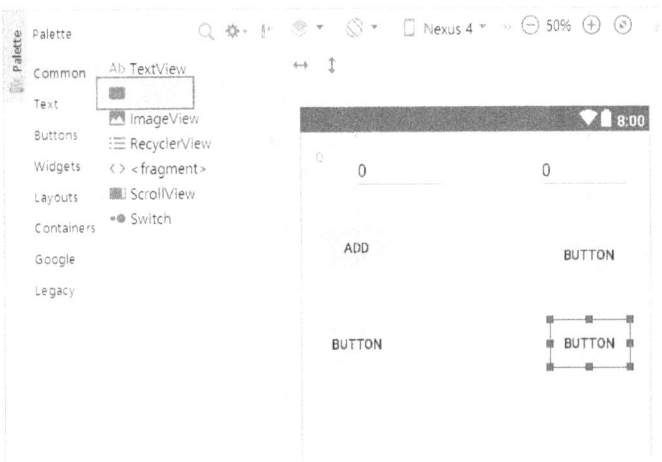

Change the attributes of the three newly added buttons as follows:
〈 The attributes of 2nd Button 〉
- onClick : onBtnMinus

- text : Minus

⟨ The attributes of 3nd Button ⟩
- onClick : onBtnMulty
- text : Multy

⟨ The attributes of 4nd Button ⟩
- onClick : onBtnDivide
- text : Divide

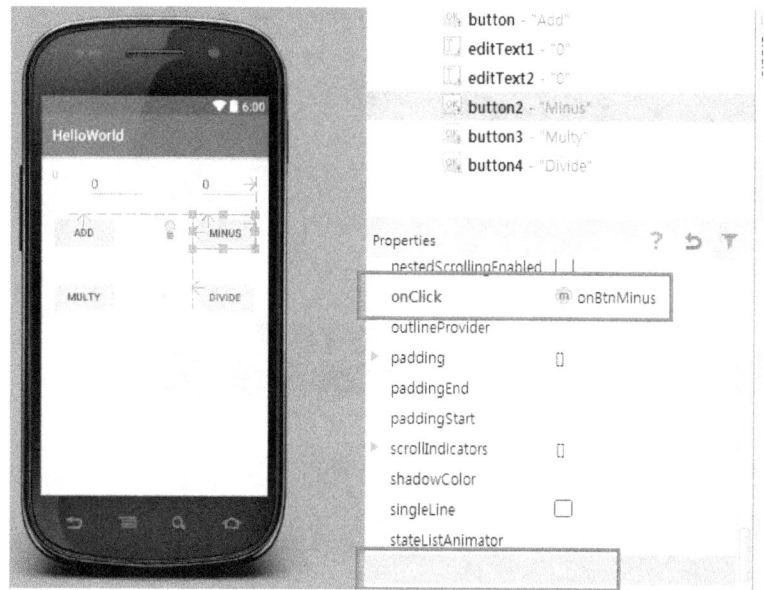

(2) Addition of two numbers in EditText
When user clicks the Add button, computer has to add the two numbers entered in EditText and display the result to the TextView. First we need to save the second EditText object in the member variable. Go back to the activity source file (MainActivity.java) and add a line of code to the beginning of the class as shown below. This code declares a member variable for the second EditText.

[Source code copy link : https://goo.gl/tHr4tT => Code-8]

```
public class MainActivity extends AppCompatActivity {
    TextView textView1;
    EditText editText1;
    EditText editText2;
```

Save the EditText widget to a newly added variable so you can use it anywhere. Add new code to the end of the onCreate () function.

[Source code copy link : https://goo.gl/tHr4tT => Code-9]

```java
protected void onCreate(Bundle savedInstanceState) {
    super.onCreate(savedInstanceState);
    setContentView(R.layout.activity_main);
    textView1 = (TextView)findViewById(R.id.textView1);
    editText1 = (EditText)findViewById(R.id.editText1);
    editText2 = (EditText)findViewById(R.id.editText2);
}
```

When the user clicks the Add button, computer reads the contents of the two EditTexts, changes them to numbers, and then performs the addition calculation and displays the result in the TextView. First, we need to clear the contents of the Add button event function as follows.

```java
public void onBtnAdd(View v) {

}
```

Then enter the required code as shown below.

[Source code copy link : https://goo.gl/tHr4tT => Code-10]

```java
public void onBtnAdd(View v) {
    String strNum = editText1.getText().toString();
    int nNum1 = Integer.parseInt(strNum);
    strNum = editText2.getText().toString();
    int nNum2 = Integer.parseInt(strNum);
    int result = nNum1 + nNum2;
    strNum = Integer.toString(result);
    textView1.setText(strNum);
}
```

Above codes means take the first EditText widget string, changed it to a number, and changed the contents of the second EditText widget to a number in the same way. Then add the two numbers, change the result to string type, and then display it in the TextView.

Let's run the example to see the result. Enter two numbers in the two EditTexts and press the Add button. The sum of the two numbers is displayed in the TextView.

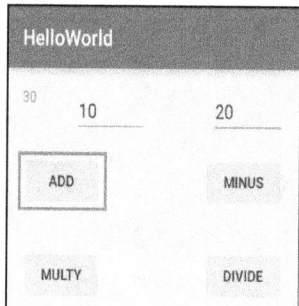

(3) Subtract, multiply, and divide two numbers in EditText

This time, we will make the functions when the subtract, multiply, and divide buttons are pressed in the same way. Create three new functions below the onBtnAdd () function.

[Source code copy link : https://goo.gl/tHr4tT => Code-11]

```java
public void onBtnAdd(View v) {
    ~
}

public void onBtnMinus(View v) {
    String strNum = editText1.getText().toString();
    int nNum1 = Integer.parseInt(strNum);
    strNum = editText2.getText().toString();
    int nNum2 = Integer.parseInt(strNum);
    int result = nNum1 - nNum2;
    strNum = Integer.toString(result);
    textView1.setText(strNum);
}

public void onBtnMulty(View v) {
    String strNum = editText1.getText().toString();
    int nNum1 = Integer.parseInt(strNum);
    strNum = editText2.getText().toString();
    int nNum2 = Integer.parseInt(strNum);
    int result = nNum1 * nNum2;
    strNum = Integer.toString(result);
    textView1.setText(strNum);
}
```

```
    public void onBtnDivide(View v) {
        String strNum = editText1.getText().toString();
        int nNum1 = Integer.parseInt(strNum);
        strNum = editText2.getText().toString();
        int nNum2 = Integer.parseInt(strNum);
        int result = nNum1 / nNum2;
        strNum = Integer.toString(result);
        textView1.setText(strNum);
    }
}
```

onBtnMinus () is an event function that is executed when the Minus button is clicked. Below is a code that subtracts two numbers.

```
        int result = nNum1 - nNum2;
```

onBtnMulty () is an event function that is executed when the Multy button is clicked. Below is a code that multiplies two numbers.

```
        int result = nNum1 * nNum2;
```

onBtnDivide () is an event function that is executed when the Divide button is clicked. Below is a code that divides two numbers.

```
        int result = nNum1 / nNum2;
```

Let's run the example to see the results. Enter two numbers in the two EditTexts and press the buttons one by one.
Press the Minus button displays the result of subtraction.
Press the Multy button displays the result of multiplication.
Press the Divide button displays the result of division.

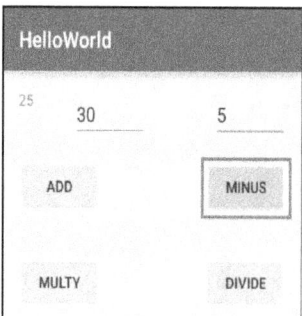
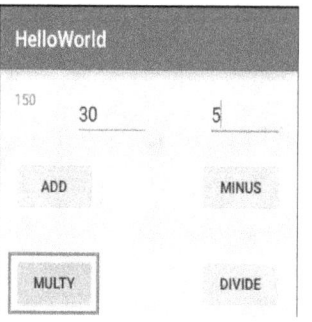
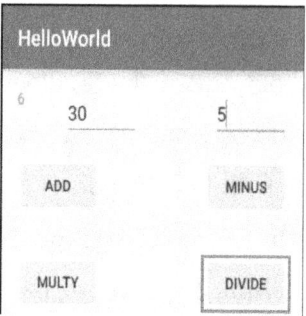

The complete code for this example is shown below. Thank you.

```java
package com.example.helloworld;
import android.support.v7.app.AppCompatActivity;
import android.os.Bundle;
import android.view.View;
import android.widget.EditText;
import android.widget.TextView;

public class MainActivity extends AppCompatActivity {
    TextView textView1;
    EditText editText1;
    EditText editText2;

    @Override
    protected void onCreate(Bundle savedInstanceState) {
        super.onCreate(savedInstanceState);
        setContentView(R.layout.activity_main);
        textView1 = (TextView)findViewById(R.id.textView1);
        editText1 = (EditText)findViewById(R.id.editText1);
        editText2 = (EditText)findViewById(R.id.editText2);
    }

    public void onBtnAdd(View v) {
        String strNum = editText1.getText().toString();
        int nNum1 = Integer.parseInt(strNum);
        strNum = editText2.getText().toString();
        int nNum2 = Integer.parseInt(strNum);
```

```java
        int result = nNum1 + nNum2;
        strNum = Integer.toString(result);
        textView1.setText(strNum);
    }


    public void onBtnMinus(View v) {
        String strNum = editText1.getText().toString();
        int nNum1 = Integer.parseInt(strNum);
        strNum = editText2.getText().toString();
        int nNum2 = Integer.parseInt(strNum);
        int result = nNum1 - nNum2;
        strNum = Integer.toString(result);
        textView1.setText(strNum);
    }


    public void onBtnMulty(View v) {
        String strNum = editText1.getText().toString();
        int nNum1 = Integer.parseInt(strNum);
        strNum = editText2.getText().toString();
        int nNum2 = Integer.parseInt(strNum);
        int result = nNum1 * nNum2;
        strNum = Integer.toString(result);
        textView1.setText(strNum);
    }


    public void onBtnDivide(View v) {
        String strNum = editText1.getText().toString();
        int nNum1 = Integer.parseInt(strNum);
        strNum = editText2.getText().toString();
        int nNum2 = Integer.parseInt(strNum);
        int result = nNum1 / nNum2;
        strNum = Integer.toString(result);
        textView1.setText(strNum);
    }
```

```
}
```

[Exercise] EditText & Number-squared operation

1. Create a new source project and set name to 'SquareOperation'
Create a TextView, EditTex, and Button widget in the layout file.

2. When user enter a number in EditText and click the button, display the caption text of EditText in the TextView.

3. When user clicks the button, calculate the square of the value entered in EditText and display it in the TextView

Ex) Input : 3 / Output : 9
    Input : 4 / Output : 16

H. BMI (Body Mass Index) calculator

This time, let's create an example that calculates BMI (Body mass index). When the BMI value is 26, the likelihood of getting diabetes is 8 times for women and 4 times for men compared to 21 people. Also, the chances of developing gallstone disease and hypertension are three times higher. The normal or abnormal range by numerical value is as follows.
- 20 under : low weight
- 20~25 : normal weight
- 25~30 : over weight
- 30~40 : obesity
- 40 over : extremely obesity

Here's how to calculate BMI: You can divide your weight by the square of the height. Here the unit of the height is meters, not cm or inch.
- BMI = weight(kg) / height(m) / height(m)

To create this example, let's look at how to use the guide text in EditText, and how to create a String by specifying format.

[Key point of this chapter]

```
# How to user EditText #
- Set guide text of EditText on hint property in layout file
Ex) hint : Height

# How to set format of string #
- Input integer in String : <String variable> = String.format("%d", <integer variable>);
int num = 103;
String strNum =String.format("%d", num);     // strNum : "103"
- Input real number in String : <String variable> = String.format("%f", <real number variable>);
double pie = 3.141592653589793;
String strNum =String.format("%f", pie);     // strNum : "3.14159"
- Set number of decimal places in String : <String variable> = String.format("%.<number of decimal places>f", <real number variable>);
double pie = 3.141592653589793;
String strNum =String.format("%.2f", pie);     // strNum : "3.14"
```

1) Screen layout configuration

(1) Create new source project
We will create a new source project. Select main menu [File > New > New Project…].

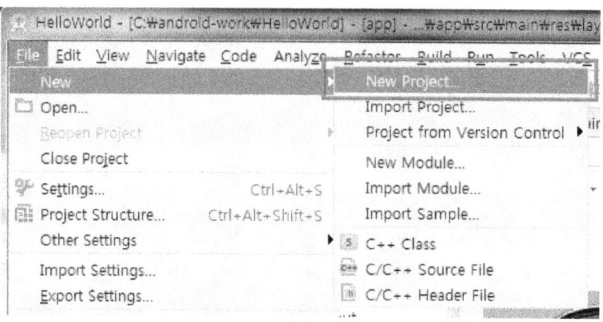

Set name of project to 'MyBMI' and click the 'Next' button. After that, it is the same as creating the source project previous.

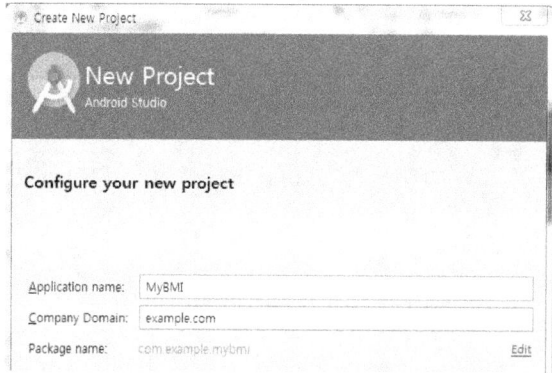

(2) Create widget in Layout file
Let's add a widget to the screen. Go to the layout information file (activity_main.xml) and change '~.Constraint Layout' to 'RelativeLayout' in Text editing mode. Then return to Design editing mode again.
Change the properties of the TextView as shown below.
〈TextView〉
- id : textView1
- text : 0

We will create two EditTexts and one Button widget. If you want to use HelloWorld source project, delete all the buttons and create a new button.
Add three widgets and change the properties of each widget as shown below.

〈1st EditText〉

- layout:width : 80dp
- hint : Height
- id : editText1
- text : (Delete content)

〈2nd EditText〉
- layout:width : 80dp
- id : editText2
- hint : Weight
- text : (Delete content)

〈Button〉
- onClick : onBtnResult
- text : Result

In EditText, delete the contents of the text property, and enter 'Height' and 'Weight' for the hint property. The hint attribute specifies the guide text. When there is no content in EditText, the guide text appears in gray. Because the smartphone screen is small, the guide text is used to display a lot of information in limited space.

You can also copy the layout information codes. Press the Text button to the right of the Design button at the bottom of the screen and go to text editing mode. When the layout text editing mode appears, delete all the contents and enter the following code.
In Design mode, you can create a widget with a mouse click, or type in the text editing mode. The result of using either method is the same.

[Source code copy link : https://goo.gl/vFm4A4 => Code-1]

```xml
<?xml version="1.0" encoding="utf-8"?>
<RelativeLayout xmlns:android="http://schemas.android.com/apk/res/android"
    xmlns:tools="http://schemas.android.com/tools"
    android:layout_width="match_parent"
    android:layout_height="match_parent"
    android:padding="20dp">

    <TextView
        android:layout_width="wrap_content"
        android:layout_height="wrap_content"
        android:text="0"
        android:id="@+id/textView1" />

    <EditText
        android:layout_width="80dp"
        android:layout_height="wrap_content"
        android:id="@+id/editText1"
        android:layout_toEndOf="@+id/textView1"
        android:layout_marginStart="36dp"
        android:hint="Height" />

    <EditText
        android:layout_width="80dp"
        android:layout_height="wrap_content"
        android:id="@+id/editText2"
        android:layout_alignParentEnd="true"
        android:hint="Weight" />

    <Button
        android:layout_width="wrap_content"
        android:layout_height="wrap_content"
        android:text="Result"
        android:layout_marginTop="37dp"
```

```
            android:layout_below="@+id/editText1"
            android:onClick="onBtnResult" />
</RelativeLayout>
```

Let's run the example in this state. If there is no content in EditText, the guide text will appear in gray. The string you entered in the hint attribute is an informative phrase. Let's enter a string in EditText. The guide text disappears and the string you entered is displayed.

2) Write the source code

We will declare the widget as a member variable to input the user's information and output the result. Go to the activity source file (MainActivity.java) and add the following new code below the beginning of the class. If you see a red letter, press the keyboard shortcut Alt + Enter.

[Source code copy link : https://goo.gl/vFm4A4 => Code-2]

```
public class MainActivity extends AppCompatActivity {
    TextView textView1;
    EditText editText1;
    EditText editText2;
```

We have declared three member variables to store a TextView and two EditTexts.

We will save the widgets to the above variables. Add the following new code to the end of onCreate () function.

[Source code copy link : https://goo.gl/vFm4A4 => Code-3]

```
protected void onCreate(Bundle savedInstanceState) {
        super.onCreate(savedInstanceState);
        setContentView(R.layout.activity_main);
        textView1 = (TextView)findViewById(R.id.textView1);
        editText1 = (EditText)findViewById(R.id.editText1);
        editText2 = (EditText)findViewById(R.id.editText2);
    }
```

When user clicks the Result button, computer will calculate the height and weight and display the body mass index on the screen. Create a new function under the onCreate () function and name the function onBtnResult ().

[Source code copy link : https://goo.gl/vFm4A4 => Code-4]

```java
public void onBtnResult(View v) {
    String strNum = editText1.getText().toString();
    double height = Integer.parseInt(strNum);
    strNum = editText2.getText().toString();
    double weight = Integer.parseInt(strNum);
    double result = weight / height / height * 10000;
    strNum = Double.toString(result);
    textView1.setText(strNum);
}
```

The height value is obtained from the first EditText, and the weight value is from the second EditText. The body mass index is calculated and displayed in the TextView.

Below is the code for calculating body mass index. When calculating the body mass index, change the height value from cm unit to meter, get the squared value, and divide it by weight value. If you want to change the unit of cm in meter, you have to divide it by 100. In this case, it is divided into 10,000 because square is used. Since we divide the height in weight, multiplying it by 10,000 is equivalent to dividing the height by 10000.

```java
double result = weight / height / height * 10000;
```

Here is the code that changes a double to a String type to display the result in the TextView. Integer.toString () is a function that converts an integer type to a string, Double.toString () is a function that changes a double type to a string.

```java
strNum = Double.toString(result);
```

Let's run the example and check the results. If you enter your height and weight and press the Result button, your body mass index will be displayed in the TextView.

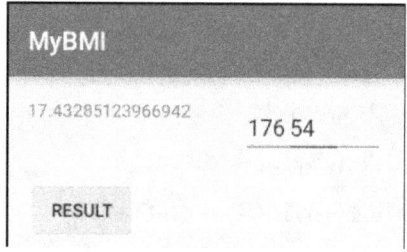

But there is something unnatural. The number of decimal places in the result is too long. Let's modify it to display only the second decimal place appropriately. In the onBtnResult () function, place the '//' sign before the co de that changes the result value to a string.

```java
public void onBtnResult(View v) {
    String strNum = editText1.getText().toString();
    double height = Integer.parseInt(strNum);
    strNum = editText2.getText().toString();
    double weight = Integer.parseInt(strNum);
    double result = weight / height / height * 10000;
    //strNum = Double.toString(result);
    textView1.setText(strNum);
}
```

'//' means change a code to a comment. Comment is the addition of a description about the source code between the codes. This ensures that comments are not included in the executable file when compiled.

We've commented out the code that changes the result value to a string, so we need a new code. Add the following new code to the onBtnResult () function:

[Source code copy link : https://goo.gl/vFm4A4 => Code-5]

```java
public void onBtnResult(View v) {
    String strNum = editText1.getText().toString();
    double height = Integer.parseInt(strNum);
    strNum = editText2.getText().toString();
    double weight = Integer.parseInt(strNum);
    double result = weight / height / height * 10000;
    //strNum = Double.toString(result);
    strNum = String.format("%.2f", result);
    textView1.setText(strNum);
}
```

String.format () is a function that creates a string by specifying a format. The symbols used in the string format statement are as follows.
- %f : Assign a real number value to this position.
- %.2f : Assign a real number value to this position and displays only the second decimal place.
- %d : Assign an integer value to this position.
- %s: Assign a string to this position.

The number stored in the result variable is changed to a string, so under the second decimal place is discarded and the rest is stored in strNum.

Let's run the example again and check the result. Enter the height and weight. And click the Result button, only the second decimal place is displayed.

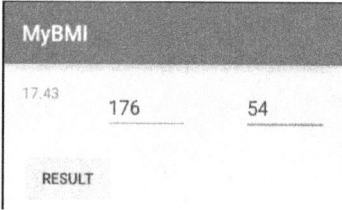

The complete code for this example is shown below. Thank you.

```java
package com.example.mybmi;
import android.support.v7.app.AppCompatActivity;
import android.os.Bundle;
import android.view.View;
import android.widget.EditText;
import android.widget.TextView;

public class MainActivity extends AppCompatActivity {
    TextView textView1;
    EditText editText1;
    EditText editText2;

    @Override
    protected void onCreate(Bundle savedInstanceState) {
        super.onCreate(savedInstanceState);
        setContentView(R.layout.activity_main);
        textView1 = (TextView)findViewById(R.id.textView1);
        editText1 = (EditText)findViewById(R.id.editText1);
        editText2 = (EditText)findViewById(R.id.editText2);
    }

    public void onBtnResult(View v) {
        String strNum = editText1.getText().toString();
        double height = Integer.parseInt(strNum);
        strNum = editText2.getText().toString();
        double weight = Integer.parseInt(strNum);
```

```
        double result = weight / height / height * 10000;
        //strNum = Double.toString(result);
        strNum = String.format("%.2f", result);
        textView1.setText(strNum);
    }
}
```

[Exercise] Change unit of BMI calculator

Change Height unit to inch in BMI calculator.
Change Weight unit to pound.
Tip : 1inch = 2.54cm
     1pound = 0.453592 kg

[Exercise] Broca's Index calculator

* Prior knowledge: The Broca's index is a way to calculate the weight for a height.
Subtract 100 from the height (cm), and then multiply by 0.9.

1. Create a new source project and create One TextView, One EditTex, and One Button widget in the layout file.

2. When Click the button, get the value entered in EditText, subtract 100, then multiply by 0.9.
Then display the result in the TextView.

I. If - else conditional statement

This time, let's create an example that gets the maximum and minimum values when the user enters three numbers. To implement this functionality, you must be able to use conditional statement. Among the coding grammars, conditional statement is the most commonly used grammar.

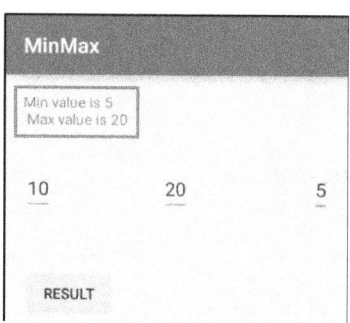

[Key point of this chapter]

```
# How to use if conditional statement #
- if conditional statement :
if ( <conditional statement> ) {
<source code runned when conditional statement is true>
}
Ex)
if( 3 > 1 ) {          // This conditional statement is true
     textView1.setText("3 > 1 is true");    // This code is runned
}

# Type of compare operator #
- Left value is bigger than right value : >
- Left value is smaller than right value : <
- Left value is bigger than or equal to right value : >=
- Left value is smaller than or equal to right value : <=
- Left value is equal to right value : ==
- Left value is different with right value : !=
```

1) if statement – in case true

(1) Create a new source project
Let's look at an example to see how to use conditional statement. We will create a new source project. Name the project 'MinMax'.

(2) Create widgets in Layout file
Let's add a widget to the screen. Go to the layout information file (activity_main.xml) and change '~.Constraint Layout' to 'RelativeLayout' in Text editing mode. Then return to Design editing mode again.
Change the properties of the automatically generated TextView as shown below.
〈TextView〉
- id : textView1
- text : Input Value

We will create three EditTexts and one Button widget below it.

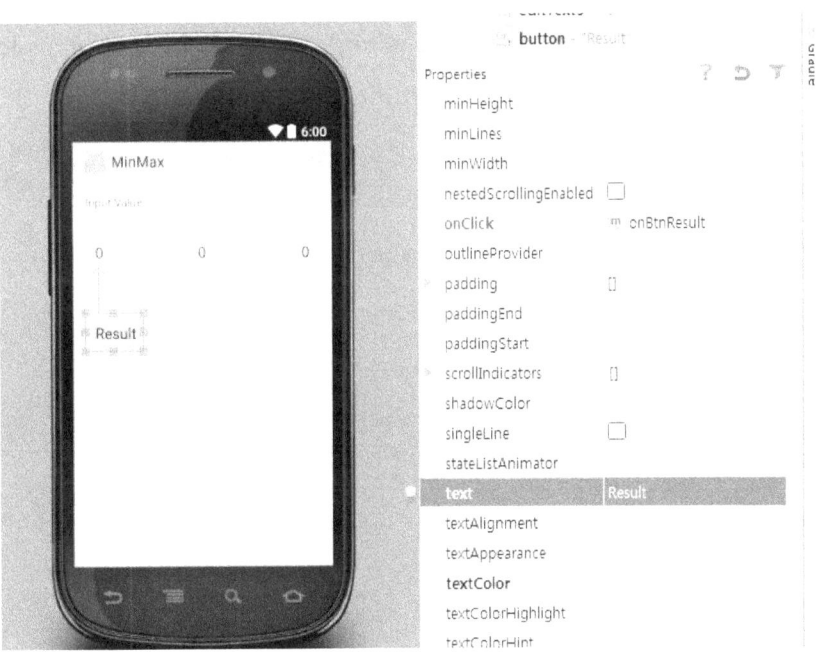

Change the properties of each widget as shown below.

〈1st EditText〉
- layout:width : 80dp
- id : editText1
- text : 0

〈2nd EditText〉
- layout:width : 80dp
- id : editText2
- text : 0

〈3rd EditText〉
- layout:width : 80dp
- id : editText3

- text : 0

〈Button〉
- onClick : onBtnResult
- text : Result

You can also copy the layout information codes. Press the Text button to the right of the Design button at the bottom of the screen and go to text editing mode. When the layout text editing mode appears, delete all the contents and enter the following code.

[Source code copy link : https://goo.gl/knVyxg => Code-1]

```xml
<?xml version="1.0" encoding="utf-8"?>
<RelativeLayout xmlns:android="http://schemas.android.com/apk/res/android"
    xmlns:tools="http://schemas.android.com/tools"
    android:layout_width="match_parent"
    android:layout_height="match_parent"
    android:padding="20dp">

    <TextView
        android:layout_width="wrap_content"
        android:layout_height="wrap_content"
        android:text="Input Value"
        android:id="@+id/textView1" />

    <EditText
        android:layout_width="wrap_content"
        android:layout_height="wrap_content"
        android:id="@+id/editText1"
        android:layout_below="@+id/textView1"
        android:layout_alignParentStart="true"
        android:layout_marginTop="34dp"
        android:text="0" />

    <EditText
        android:layout_width="wrap_content"
        android:layout_height="wrap_content"
        android:id="@+id/editText2"
```

```xml
        android:text="0"
        android:layout_alignTop="@+id/editText1"
        android:layout_centerHorizontal="true" />

    <EditText
        android:layout_width="wrap_content"
        android:layout_height="wrap_content"
        android:id="@+id/editText3"
        android:text="0"
        android:layout_alignTop="@+id/editText2"
        android:layout_alignParentEnd="true" />

    <Button
        android:layout_width="wrap_content"
        android:layout_height="wrap_content"
        android:text="Result"
        android:id="@+id/button"
        android:layout_below="@+id/editText1"
        android:layout_alignParentStart="true"
        android:layout_marginTop="53dp"
        android:onClick="onBtnResult" />
</RelativeLayout>
```

(3) Compare numbers by source code

We will declare the widgets as a member variable in order to get user input and output the result. Go to the Activity source file (MainActivity.java) and add the following new code below the beginning of the class. If a red letter is displayed, press the shortcut key Alt + Enter.

[Source code copy link : https://goo.gl/knVyxg => Code-2]

```java
public class MainActivity extends AppCompatActivity {
    TextView textView1;
    EditText editText1;
    EditText editText2;
    EditText editText3;
```

We have declared member variables to store one TextView and three EditTexts.
We will save the widgets to the above variables. Add the following new code to the onCreate () function.

[Source code copy link : https://goo.gl/knVyxg => Code-3]

```java
protected void onCreate(Bundle savedInstanceState) {
    super.onCreate(savedInstanceState);
    setContentView(R.layout.activity_main);
    textView1 = (TextView)findViewById(R.id.textView1);
    editText1 = (EditText)findViewById(R.id.editText1);
    editText2 = (EditText)findViewById(R.id.editText2);
    editText3 = (EditText)findViewById(R.id.editText3);
}
```

When user clicks the Result button, computer will display the result if the formula 3 > 1 is true. Create a new function under the onCreate () function and name it onBtnResult ().

[Source code copy link : https://goo.gl/knVyxg => Code-4]

```java
public void onBtnResult(View v) {
    if( 3 > 1 )
        textView1.setText("3 > 1 is true");
}
```

'if' is a command that determines if a condition is true or false. In the code below, if the condition A is true, the code B is executed. If A is false, B is not executed.

```
if( A )
   B
```

The '>' sign means the left value is bigger than the right. So in the source code 3 is bigger than 1, and the next line is executed. If the condition statement is false, the next line is skipped.

Press the keyboard shortcut Ctrl + s to save the changes and run the example. Clicking the button will change the TextView string. 3 is bigger than 1, so the if conditional is true, and the text '3> 1 is true' is displayed in the TextView.

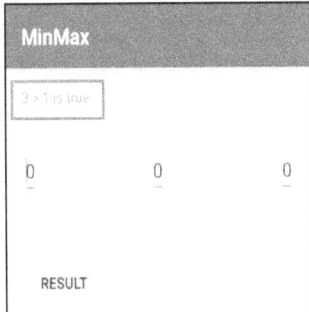

Let's look at another example of a conditional statement. Add the following new code to the onBtnResult () function.

[Source code copy link : https://goo.gl/knVyxg => Code-5]

```
public void onBtnResult(View v) {
    if( 3 > 1 )
        textView1.setText("3 > 1 is true");
    if( 4 < 2 )
        textView1.append("\n 4 < 2 is true");
    if( 5 == 5 ) {
        textView1.append("\n 5 == 5 is true");
    }
}
```

The code below is true when 4 is less than 2. The next line is not executed because it is false.

```
if( 4 < 2 )
```

In the code below, TextView.append () is a function that adds a new string to the TextView. setText () deletes the existing content and changes it to the new content, but append () leaves the existing content and appends the new content to the end.
' \ n' is a line break that goes to the next line.

```
textView1.append("\n 4 < 2 is true");
```

Below conditional statement is true when 5 is equal to 5. In most computer languages including the Java language, the '=' sign means that save the value on the right to the variable on the left, and the '==' sign means the left and right are equal.
After the condition, the code is enclosed in parentheses ({}). You can omit the parentheses if the conditional is true and the code to execute is only one line. If you need to perform multiple lines, you must enclose them in parentheses.

```
        if( 5 == 5 ) {
            textView1.append("\n 5 == 5 is true");
        }
```

Let's run the example again. When you click the button, a 2-line string is displayed in the TextView.

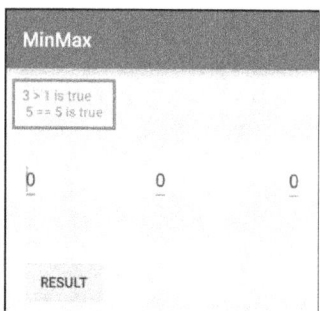

The string corresponding to the result of the first and third conditional statements was displayed. The result of the second condition query is invisible. 3 > 1 and 5 == 5 is true, and 4 < 2 is false.

2) if-else condition statement – in case false

(1) if ~ else ~ Use of conditional statement
We have seen how to execute the desired code when the if conditional statement is true. This time, let's look at how to execute the desired code when the conditional statement is false. First, delete the contents of the onBtnResult () function as shown below.

```
    public void onBtnResult(View v) {


    }
```

Then enter the new code in the onBtnResult () function as shown below.

[Source code copy link : https://goo.gl/knVyxg => Code-6]

```
  public void onBtnResult(View v) {
        int num1 = 10, num2 = 20;
        if( num1 != 10 )
            textView1.setText("num1 == 10 is false");
        else {
            textView1.setText("num1 == 10 is true");
        }
```

```
      }
```

The following code creates two integer variables, initializing the first variable to 10, and the second variable to 20.

```
      int num1 = 10, num2 = 20;
```

Below is a conditional statement that is true when num1 and 10 are different. '==' means that the two values are the same, and '!=' Means that the two values are different.

```
      if( num1 != 10 )
```

Below is the code that executes when the if conditional statement is not true. When the if condition is true the next code is executed, and when the opposite the code after the else condition is executed.

```
      else {
          textView1.setText("num1 == 10 is true");
```

Let's run the example to see the result. When you press the Button, the string 'num1 == 10 is true' is displayed.

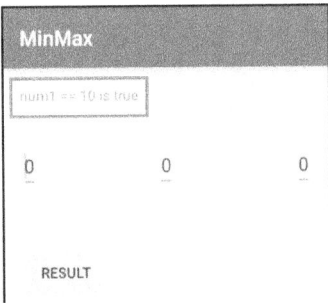

Since num1 is 10, the following conditional statement is false. Therefore, the query code of the if condition statement is not executed and the result code of the else condition statement is executed.

```
      if( num1 != 10 )
```

[Tip] The types of comparison operators used in conditional statements are:
- 〉 : True if the left value is bigger than the right value
- 〈 : True if the left value is less than right value
- 〉= : True if the left value is bigger than or equal to the right value
- 〈= : True if the left value is less than or equal to the right value
- == : True if left value equals right
- != : True if left value is different from right
- && : True only if left and right are both true
- || : True one or more of the left and the right is true

(2) Use of 'else if ~ ' conditional statement

The if - else conditional statements can be divided into two cases to perform an action. However, let's look at how to perform the operation in three cases, when the value of the variable A is bigger than 20, when it is less than 20, and when it is 20.

You can use else - if. In the code below, if B is true, the C statement is executed; otherwise, if D is true the E statement is executed. If D is false, then the F statement is executed.

```
if( B )
    C
else if( D )
    E
else
    F
```

Let's check it through practice. Add the following new code to the onBtnResult () function.

[Source code copy link : https://goo.gl/knVyxg => Code-7]

```java
public void onBtnResult(View v) {
    int num1 = 10, num2 = 20;
    if( num1 != 10 )
        textView1.setText("num1 == 10 is false");
    else {
        textView1.setText("num1 == 10 is true");
        if( num2 < 20 )
            textView1.append("\n num2 < 20 is true");
        else if( num2 == 20 )
            textView1.append("\n num2 == 20 is true");
        else
            textView1.append("\n num2 > 20 is true");
    }
}
```

The second if - else code is added in the execute code of the first else statement '{ }'. It is also possible to include the if statement in the if statement. Computers are not confusing, but people could get confused. Use complex functions that go beyond three levels to create new functions.

Below is the newly added code. If num2 is less than 20, the text 'num2 <20 is true' is added to the TextView. If not, computer checks whether num2 is 20, and if it is true, the text 'num2 == 20 is true' is displayed. If this is also false, the last thing 'num2> 20 is true' is displayed.

```
        if( num2 < 20 )
            textView1.append("\n num2 < 20 is true");
        else if( num2 == 20 )
            textView1.append("\n num2 == 20 is true");
        else
            textView1.append("\n num2 > 20 is true");
```

Let's run the example again and check the results. When the button is pressed, a 2-line string is displayed in the TextView. Since the contents of the second line are displayed as 'num2 == 20 is true', the execute code of 'else if' is executed in the above code.

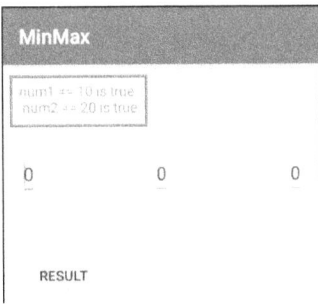

[Exercise] if, else conditional statement
1. Create a new source project and set name to 'SmallBig'.
Create a TextView, EditText, and Button widget in the layout file.

2. When user click the button, get the value entered in EditText.
If it is smaller than 10, display the text 'Small' in the TextView.

3. If the value entered in EditText is 10 or more,
display the text 'Big' in the TextView.

[Exercise] Show rating in BMI calculator application
* Prior knowledge: 'Law weight' if 'BMI' is below 20.
'Normal' if less than 25. 'Overweight' if less than 30,
'Obesity' if less than 40, and 'Extremly obesity' if higher than 40.

1. Load the MyBMI example you created earlier, and display the rating on the screen using the if - else conditional statement. For example, if the BMI index is 25.7, you might say "25.7 - overweight" in the TextView.

J. Get Maximum & Minumun

[Key point of this chapter]

```
# How to use if – else #
- if else if conditional statement :
if ( < conditional statement 1> ) {
< Source code when conditional statement 1 is true >
} else if ( < conditional statement 2 > ) {
< Source code when conditional statement 2 is true >
} else {
< Source code when conditional statement 1& 2 both are false >
}
Ex)
if( 3 == 1 ) {         // conditional statement -1
    textView1.setText("3 and 1 is equal");    // Run when only conditional statement -1 is true
} else if( 3 < 1 ) {    // conditional statement -2
textView1.setText("3 is smaller than 1");   // Run when only conditional statement -2 is true
} else {
textView1.setText("3 is bigger than 1");    // Run when conditional statement 1& 2 both are false
}

# Type of complex operator #
- True only both left and right are true : &&
Ex) if( 3> 1 && 5 < 7 )     // left: true, right: true, total: true
    if( 4<=6 && 3 == 4)     // left: true, right: false, total: false
if( 4!=4 && 3 > 4)     // left: false, right: false, total: false

- True when one of two are true : ||
Ex) if( 3> 1 && 5 < 7 )     // left: true, right: true, total: true
    if( 4<=6 && 3 == 4)     // left: true, right: false, total: true
if( 4!=4 && 3 > 4)     // left: false, right: false, total: false
```

1) Getting the Minimum value

Let's implement the ability to find the smallest number of three numbers user enter. To do this, delete the code entered in the onBtnResult () function as shown below.

```
public void onBtnResult(View v) {
```

```
    }
```

Then enter the new code as shown below.

[Source code copy link : https://goo.gl/knVyxg => Code-8]

```
    public void onBtnResult(View v) {
        int num1, num2, num3, min, max;
        String strNum = editText1.getText().toString();
        num1 = Integer.parseInt(strNum);
        strNum = editText2.getText().toString();
        num2 = Integer.parseInt(strNum);
        strNum = editText3.getText().toString();
        num3 = Integer.parseInt(strNum);
        min = max = num1;

        if( num1 > num2 && num3 > num2 )
            min = num2;
        else if(num1 > num3 && num2 > num3)
            min = num3;
        textView1.setText("Min value is " + min);
    }
```

The first line of the newly added code declares five integer variables. Let num1, num2, and num3 contain the contents of EditText. min stores the smallest of the three values, and max stores the largest of the three.
After then read the three EditText strings, convert them to integer numbers, and store them in variables.

Below is the code that initializes the minimum and maximum variables to the value of the first EditText. A = B = C means to store C value in A and B.

```
    min = max = num1;
```

Below is a conditional statement to determine if num2 is the smallest value. if (A && B) is true when both A and B are true. To be true even if only one of A and B is true, you can use '||'.
If num1 > num2 is true, num2 is smaller than num1, and if num3 > num2 is true, num2 is smaller than num3, so num2 is the minimum value.

```
        if( num1 > num2 && num3 > num2 )
            min = num2;
```

If num2 is not the minimum value, the execute code of the above conditional statement is not executed. If so, you need to determine if num3 is the minimum value. At that case the code below is executed.
If num1 > num3 is true, then num3 is less than num1, and if num2 > num3 is true, num3 is less than num2, so num3 is the minimum value.

```
else if(num1 > num3 && num2 > num3)
    min = num3;
```

If num2 is not the minimum value and num3 is not the minimum value either, the above two conditional statements will not execute any result code in parenthesis. Since num1 is stored in min, num1 automatically becomes the minimum value.
Let's run the example and enter the numbers into three EditTexts. Then press the button to display the minimum value in the TextView.

2) Getting the Maximum value

Now we got the minimum value, we will try to get the maximum value. Enter the new code at the end of the onBtnResult () function as shown below. This code gets the maximum of the three numbers and appends the result to the TextView.

[Source code copy link : https://goo.gl/knVyxg => Code-9]

```
public void onBtnResult(View v) {

    ~

    if( num1 > num2 && num3 > num2 )
        min = num2;
    else if(num1 > num3 && num2 > num3)
        min = num3;
    textView1.setText("Min value is " + min);
```

```
        if( max < num2 )
            max = num2;
        if( max < num3 )
            max = num3;
        textView1.append("\n Max value is " + max);
    }
```

This time we used the if conditional statement twice instead of if – else. Whichever method you use, the result is the same. Below is a code that stores num2 in max if num2 is bigger than the value stored in max. The value bigger than num1 is remembered.

```
        if( max < num2 )
            max = num2;
```

Below is a code that stores num3 in max if num3 is bigger than the value stored in max. Finally, the biggest value is stored in max.

```
        if( max < num3 )
            max = num3;
```

Let's run the example and enter the numbers in EditText. Then press the button and the TextView will display a 2-line string. The second line shows the maximum value.

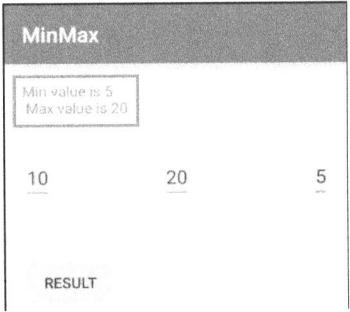

The example to get the maximum and minimum values is complete. The complete code for this example is shown below. Thank you.

```
package com.example.minmax;

import android.support.v7.app.AppCompatActivity;

import android.os.Bundle;

import android.view.View;

import android.widget.EditText;
```

```java
import android.widget.TextView;

public class MainActivity extends AppCompatActivity {
    TextView textView1;
    EditText editText1;
    EditText editText2;
    EditText editText3;

    @Override
    protected void onCreate(Bundle savedInstanceState) {
        super.onCreate(savedInstanceState);
        setContentView(R.layout.activity_main);
        textView1 = (TextView)findViewById(R.id.textView1);
        editText1 = (EditText)findViewById(R.id.editText1);
        editText2 = (EditText)findViewById(R.id.editText2);
        editText3 = (EditText)findViewById(R.id.editText3);
    }

    public void onBtnResult(View v) {
        int num1, num2, num3, min, max;
        String strNum = editText1.getText().toString();
        num1 = Integer.parseInt(strNum);
        strNum = editText2.getText().toString();
        num2 = Integer.parseInt(strNum);
        strNum = editText3.getText().toString();
        num3 = Integer.parseInt(strNum);
        min = max = num1;

        if( num1 > num2 && num3 > num2 )
            min = num2;
        else if(num1 > num3 && num2 > num3)
            min = num3;
        textView1.setText("Min value is " + min);
```

```
            if( max < num2 )
                max = num2;
            if( max < num3 )
                max = num3;
            textView1.append("\n Max value is " + max);
    }
}
```

[Exercise] Determining a 2-digit number

1. Open source project named 'SmallBig' which you made in previous exercise.

2. If the value entered in EditText is bigger than 100, display the text 'Big' in the TextView.

3. If the value entered in EditText is bigger than 10 and smaller than 100, display the text 'Mid' in the TextView. If it is smaller than 10, display the word 'Small'.

K. Create Random number & boolean variable

This time, let's create an example where the computer randomly chooses one of the pairs, and the user presses one of the two buttons to display the result on the screen. To implement this functionality, you must be able to generate random numbers and know how to use the boolean variable.

[Key point of this chapter]

```
# How to user boolean variable #
- The data can stores in boolean variable are only two : true, false
Ex)
boolean bHandsome = true;      // he is handsome
boolean bHandsome = false;     // he is ugly


# Create a random number #
- Real random number generate function between 0 and 1 : Math.random()
- Integer random number generator between 1 and 3
  int rand = (int)(Math.random() * 3) + 1;    // rand : one of 1, 2 or 3
```

1) boolean variable

(1) Create new source project
A random number, like dice, is the computer's choice of a number in a range. You do not know what numbers are coming out. Most games use random numbers frequently. Let's look at how to create a random number through the example. Create a new source project. Set name the project to 'OddEven'.

(2) Make widget in Layout file
Let's add a widget to the screen. Go to the layout information file (activity_main.xml) and change the properties of the automatically generated TextView as shown below.

⟨TextView⟩
- id : textView1
- text : Select Even or Odd

And below that create two Button widgets.

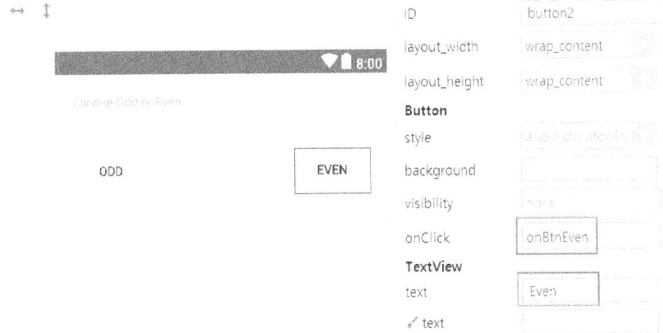

Change the properties of each Button as follows

⟨1st Button⟩
- onClick : onBtnOdd
- text : Odd

⟨2nd Button⟩
- onClick : onBtnEven
- text : Even

You can also copy the layout information codes. Press the Text button to the right of the Design button at the bottom of the screen and go to text editing mode. When the layout text editing mode appears, delete all the contents and enter the following code.

[Source code copy link : https://goo.gl/FKXVK4 => Code-1]

```xml
<?xml version="1.0" encoding="utf-8"?>
<RelativeLayout xmlns:android="http://schemas.android.com/apk/res/android"
    xmlns:tools="http://schemas.android.com/tools"
    android:layout_width="match_parent"
    android:layout_height="match_parent"
    android:padding="20dp">

    <TextView
        android:layout_width="wrap_content"
        android:layout_height="wrap_content"
        android:text="Choose Odd or Even"
        android:id="@+id/textView1" />

    <Button
        android:layout_width="wrap_content"
```

```xml
            android:layout_height="wrap_content"
            android:text="Odd"
            android:id="@+id/button"
            android:layout_below="@+id/textView1"
            android:layout_marginTop="41dp"
            android:onClick="onBtnOdd" />

        <Button
            android:layout_width="wrap_content"
            android:layout_height="wrap_content"
            android:text="Even"
            android:id="@+id/button2"
            android:layout_alignTop="@+id/button"
            android:layout_alignParentEnd="true"
            android:onClick="onBtnEven" />
</RelativeLayout>
```

(3) Initialize widget by source code
We will declare the widget as a member variable to generate a random number and output the result. Go to the activity source file (MainActivity.java) and add the following new code below the beginning of the class. If a red letter is displayed, press the shortcut key Alt + Enter.

[Source code copy link : https://goo.gl/FKXVK4 => Code-2]

```java
public class MainActivity extends AppCompatActivity {
    TextView textView1;
    boolean bOdd;
```

We have declared one TextView and one boolean as member variables. A boolean is a variable that can store only two pieces of information: true or false.

Let's save the widget to the above variable. Add the following new code to the onCreate () function.

[Source code copy link : https://goo.gl/FKXVK4 => Code-3]

```java
    protected void onCreate(Bundle savedInstanceState) {
        super.onCreate(savedInstanceState);
        setContentView(R.layout.activity_main);
        textView1 = (TextView)findViewById(R.id.textView1);
    }
```

2) Random number generation

(1) Generate Random number by math function
Now let's implement the function to create random numbers. Make a new function under the onCreate () function and name it getRandom (). Then enter the code as shown below.

[Source code copy link : https://goo.gl/FKXVK4 => Code-4]

```
public int getRandom (int max, int offset) {
        int nResult = (int)(Math.random() * max) + offset;
        return nResult;
}
```

The getRandom () function takes two parameters. The first max specifies the size of the random number range. For example, if you pass 10 to max parameter, a natural number between 0 and 9 is created. It should be noted that the number 1 less than max is the actual maximum value. This is because the minimum value is 0, not 1. The second parameter, offset is the correction value added to the generated random number. This corresponds to the minimum value. For example, passing 10 for max and 5 for offset creates a natural number between 5 and 14. The range is from 0 to 9, plus a minimum value of 5.

```
public int getRandom (int max, int offset) {
```

In the code below, Math.random () is a mathematical function that generates a random number. However, not a natural number is created, but a real number between 0 and 1.0 is created. To convert a real number to a natural number, multiply by max and cast to an integer type by using '(int)'.
When the real number is converted to an integer type, the value below the decimal point is discarded. Therefore, when max is 10, the result can not be 10. The maximum value is 9.
We added an offset to it. The minimum value is offset.

```
int nResult = (int)(Math.random() * max) + offset;
```

Below is the code that returns the newly created random number. 'return' is a command that returns a result value when the function is terminated. The value returned here must match the declaration of the function. For example, in the case of 'void onCreate ()', 'void' means 'there is nothing to return.' So the 'return' command in this function is not required.
'Int getRandom ()' means that this function returns an integer value. So you must use the 'return' command at the end of this function and return an integer value.

```
return nResult;
```

When you use the above function, you can use it as follows. This will create a number between 5 and 14 and st ore it in a variable named rand.

```
int rand = getRandom(10, 5);
```

(2) Create a random number between 0 and 9
Using the above function, pressing the 1st button, a random number between 0 and 9 is created and display it in TextView. Under the getRandom () function, make a new function and name it onBtnOdd (). Then enter the code as shown below. If you see a red letter, press the keyboard shortcut Alt + Enter.

[Source code copy link : https://goo.gl/FKXVK4 => Code-5]

```
public void onBtnOdd(View v) {
    int rand = getRandom(10, 0);
    textView1.setText("Random : " + rand);
}
```

When the user presses the first button, the above function is executed.
Use the getRandom () function to create a random number. The parameter specifies a range of 10, and a value between 0 and 9 is created because the minimum value is set to 0. The generated random number is stored in a variable named rand.
The last line is the code that displays a random number in the TextView.

Run the example and press the first button. Each time the button is pressed, a different number is displayed. No matter how many times you press it, no number less than 0 or bigger than 9 appears.

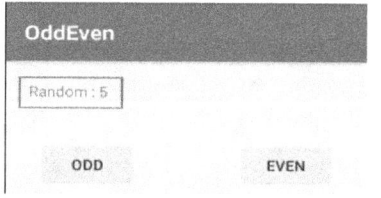
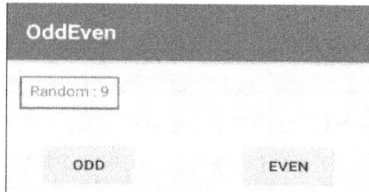

☐) Create random number by using minimum value

(1) Event function of 2nd Button
Now let's implement the function to generate the lottery number by pressing the second button. Lottery numbers are made from 1 to 45 numbers. Create a new function under the onBtnOdd () function and add the code below.

[Source code copy link : https://goo.gl/FKXVK4 => Code-6]

```
public void onBtnEven(View v) {
    int rand = getRandom(45, 1);
```

```
        textView1.setText("Lotto : " + rand);
    }
```

When the user presses the second button, the above function is executed.
Lottery number range is 45. The minimum value is 1. So when you create a random number, you pass those parameters as shown below.

```
        int rand = getRandom(45, 1);
```

Run the example again and press the second button. Each time you press the button, a new number is displayed in the TextView. No matter how many times you press them, numbers less than 1 or bigger than 45 are not displayed.

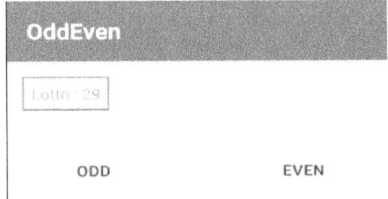

[Exercise] Create a unique number between 10 and 21

1. Create a new source project and name to 'DatingScore'. Create a TextView and Button widget in the layout file.

2. Press Button to create a unique random number between 10 and 21 and display it in TextView.

[Exercise] Making determin dating score application

1. Open the source project created above and add two EditTexts in the layout file.

2. When the user enters their name and other person's name in EditText and presses the Button, generate a random number between 0 and 100 and display it in the TextView.

3. If the random number is bigger than 80, display the following text in the TextView

"Your love score is <Random number>. You love each eather."

If the random number is less than 80 and bigger than 40, display the following text in the TextView

"Your love score is <Random number>. You just leave friend."

If the random number is 40 or less, display the following text in the TextView.

"Your love score is <Random number>. No love possiblity."

Java Coding with Android programming 1   Dennis (Donggeun Jung)

L. Even & Odd game

[Key point of this chapter]

\# How to use if – else conditional statement \#
- if else conditional statement :
if (< conditional statement >) {
<source code runned when conditional statement is true >
} else {
<source code runned when conditional statement is false >
}
Ex)
if(3 == 1) {   // This conditional statement is false
    textView1.setText("3 == 1 is true");   // This code is not runned
} else {
textView1.setText("3 == 1 is false");   // This code is runned
}

---

1) Function of Odd Button

(1) Save ture or false in boolean variable
Let's create an odd even game using the random number generation function we created last time. When user press the 'Odd' button computer will generate a random number that will be incorrect if it is 0, and be correct if it is 1.

First, clear the contents of the first Button's function as shown below.

```
public void onBtnOdd(View v) {


}
```

Then add the new code as shown below. This is a code that generates random numbers and determines odd or even number.

[Source code copy link : https://goo.gl/FKXVK4 => Code-7]

```
public void onBtnOdd(View v) {
    if( getRandom(2, 0) == 0 )
        bOdd = false;
    else
```

```
        bOdd = true;
    }
```

Below is a code that generates a random number between 0 and 1. If the random number is 0, store false in the Boolean variable to remember that the computer's choice is even.

```
    if( getRandom(2, 0) == 0 )
        bOdd = false;
```

Below is a code that stores true in the boolean variable to remember that the computer's choice is odd, if the random number is not 0. It means the random number is 1.

```
    else
        bOdd = true;
```

Now let's display the result according to the value stored in this bOdd variable. If the value of bOdd is true, the answer is correct. If it is false, it is wrong.

[Source code copy link : https://goo.gl/FKXVK4 => Code-8]

```
    public void onBtnOdd(View v) {
        if( getRandom(2, 0) == 0 )
            bOdd = false;
        else
            bOdd = true;

     if( bOdd )
            textView1.setText("Odd - Correct answer!");
        else
            textView1.setText("Wrong! The answer is Even");
    }
```

If the value of the bOdd variable is true, computer displays the string 'Odd - Correct answer!' in the TextView, and in opposite, computer displays the string 'Wrong! The answer is even'.
Save the changes, run the example and press the first button. Then the result will appears.

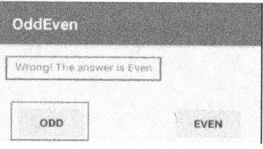 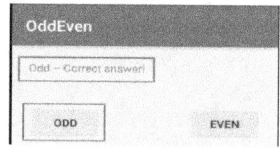

2) Function of Even Button

Let's implement the function of the even button in the same way. First, delete the contents of the second button's function as shown below.

```
public void onBtnEven(View v) {


}
```

Then add the new code as shown below. It generates random number, determines odd or even numbers, and outputs the result to the TextView.

[Source code copy link : https://goo.gl/FKXVK4 => Code-9]

```
public void onBtnEven(View v) {
 if( getRandom(2, 0) == 0 )
         bOdd = false;
     else
         bOdd = true;

     if( bOdd )
         textView1.setText("Wrong! The answer is Odd");
     else
         textView1.setText("Even - Correct answer!");
 }
```

The first part is the same as the event function of the first button. This is the event function of the even number button. So if the random number is odd, it means wrong. If the random number is even number, it means correct.
So if the value of the bOdd variable is true, computer displays the string 'Wrong! The answer is Odd' to the TextView, and in opposite, computer displays the string 'Even - Correct answer!'.
Save the changes, run the example and press the second button. Then the results will appears.

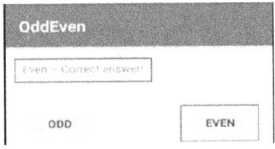 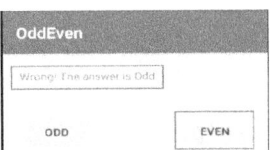

The odd-even game app is complete. This time, let's press one of the two buttons, thinking about which random number was generated.

The complete code for this example is shown below. Thank you.

```java
package com.example.oddeven;
import android.support.v7.app.AppCompatActivity;
import android.os.Bundle;
import android.view.View;
import android.widget.TextView;

public class MainActivity extends AppCompatActivity {
    TextView textView1;
    boolean bOdd;

    @Override
    protected void onCreate(Bundle savedInstanceState) {
        super.onCreate(savedInstanceState);
        setContentView(R.layout.activity_main);
        textView1 = (TextView)findViewById(R.id.textView1);
    }

    public int getRandom(int max, int offset) {
        int nResult = (int)(Math.random() * max) + offset;
        return nResult;
    }

    public void onBtnOdd(View v) {
        if( getRandom(2, 0) == 0 )
            bOdd = false;
        else
            bOdd = true;

        if( bOdd )
            textView1.setText("Odd - Correct answer!");
        else
            textView1.setText("Wrong! The answer is Even");
    }
```

```java
    public void onBtnEven(View v) {
        if( getRandom(2, 0) == 0 )
            bOdd = false;
        else
            bOdd = true;

        if( bOdd )
            textView1.setText("Wrong! The answer is Odd");
        else
            textView1.setText("Even - Correct answer!");
    }
}
```

[Exercise] Modify Odd Even game

It is a logic problem to create a random number after user press the button. Many casinos use banding machines in this way to make the game to favor themselves. So gambling can never make money for you, and you have to make a game with enjoying it for fun.

Change the way the computer selects random number first before user press Button.
1. Create a new function (void makeQuiz ()), Input codes that create a random number and store the result in the member variable (bOdd).

2. Call the makeQuiz () function under the following three conditions. (1) The first time the app is launched. (2) After display the result on the screen when the user presses the first button. (3) After display the result on the screen when the user presses the second button.

3. Modify the onBtnOdd () and onBtnEven () functions to complete the game example.

[Exercise] Rock Paper Scissors game
1. Create a new source project and set name to 'SimpleRPS'.
Create a TextView and a Button widget in the layout file.

2. When user press Button, create a unique random number between 0 and 2.

3. If the generated random number is 0, display the word 'scissors' in the TextView,
If the random number is 1, 'Rock', if 2, 'Paper' is displayed in the TextView.

4. Once you have done this, run the example,
Fist off one of the scissors, rock, or paper and press the button.
Keep trying until you win 3 times.

M. Toast message

This time, we will make a multiplication game randomly. We will use a Toast message to show the result of user input.

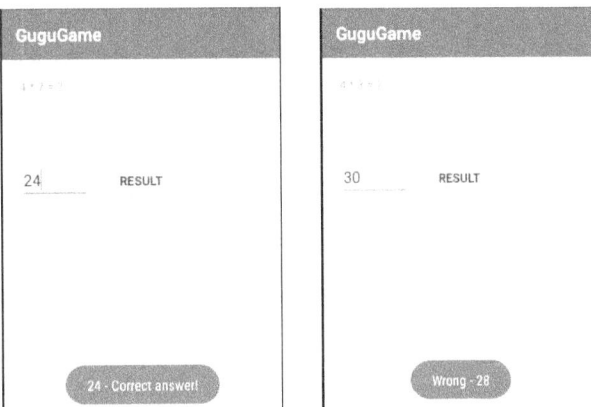

[Key point of this chapter]

How to use Toast message
- Create Toast message object : Toast.makeText(<Context object>, <message string>, <length of time>)
Ex) Toast toast = Toast.makeText(this, "This is a Toast message", Toast.LENGTH_SHORT);
- Display Toast message on screen : Toast.show();
Ex) toast.show();
- Create & display Toast message on screen: Toast.makeText(<Context object>, <message string>, <length of time>).show()
Ex) Toast.makeText(this, "This is a Toast message", Toast.LENGTH_SHORT).show();

1) Toast message display

(1) Make a new source project
On Android, you can use a message that appears at the bottom of the screen for a brief moment and disappears. This is called a Toast message. Let's make an example to show how to generate a Toast message. Create a new source project. And name the project 'GuguGame'.

(2) Make new widgets in Layout file
Let's add widgets to the screen. Go to the layout information file (activity_main.xml) and change the properties of the automatically generated TextView as shown below.
〈TextView〉
- id : textView1

And below it add one EditText and one Button widget. Find 'Plain Text' in 'Text Fields' group, that is the normal EditText widget.

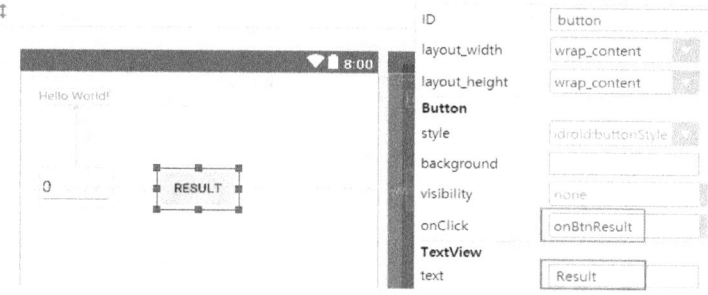

After then change the properties of each widget as shown below.

〈 EditText 〉
- layout:width : 80dp
- id : editText1
- text : 0

〈 Button 〉
- onClick : onBtnResult
- text : Result

You can also copy the layout information. Press the Text button to the right of the Design button at the bottom of the screen and go to text editing mode. When the layout texting edit mode appears, delete all the contents and enter the following code.

[Source code copy link : https://goo.gl/KgKZym => Code-1]

```xml
<?xml version="1.0" encoding="utf-8"?>
<RelativeLayout xmlns:android="http://schemas.android.com/apk/res/android"
    xmlns:tools="http://schemas.android.com/tools"
    android:layout_width="match_parent"
    android:layout_height="match_parent"
    android:padding="20dp">

    <TextView
        android:layout_width="wrap_content"
        android:layout_height="wrap_content"
        android:text="Hello World!"
        android:id="@+id/textView1" />
```

```xml
<EditText
    android:layout_width="80dp"
    android:layout_height="wrap_content"
    android:id="@+id/editText1"
    android:layout_below="@+id/textView1"
    android:layout_marginTop="73dp"
    android:text="0" />

<Button
    android:layout_width="wrap_content"
    android:layout_height="wrap_content"
    android:text="Result"
    android:id="@+id/button"
    android:layout_alignTop="@+id/editText1"
    android:layout_centerHorizontal="true"
    android:onClick="onBtnResult" />

</RelativeLayout>
```

(3) Initialize widgets by source code

We will declare the widgets as member variable to display the question in the TextView. Go to the activity source file (MainActivity.java) and add the following new code below the beginning of the class. If a red letter is displayed, press the shortcut key Alt + Enter.

[Source code copy link : https://goo.gl/KgKZym => Code-2]

```java
public class MainActivity extends AppCompatActivity {
    TextView textView1;
    EditText editText1;
    int nResult;
```

We have declared one TextView, one EditText, and one int as member variables. nResult will store the result of the multiplication calculation.

Let's save the widget objects to the above variable. Add the following new code to the end of onCreate () function.

[Source code copy link : https://goo.gl/KgKZym => Code-3]

```java
protected void onCreate(Bundle savedInstanceState) {
    super.onCreate(savedInstanceState);
    setContentView(R.layout.activity_main);
    textView1 = (TextView)findViewById(R.id.textView1);
    editText1 = (EditText)findViewById(R.id.editText1);
    makeQuiz();
}
```

TextView and EditText widgets are stored in member variables. And a function named makeQuiz () is called. This function has not yet been created, and will be able to create a new multiplication question and output it to TextView. First, let's implement the function to display a Toast message.

Create a new function under the onCreate () function and name it makeQuiz (). Then enter the new code as shown below. If a red letter is displayed, press the shortcut key Alt + Enter.

[Source code copy link : https://goo.gl/KgKZym => Code-4]

```java
public void makeQuiz() {
    Toast.makeText(this, "This is TOAST message", Toast.LENGTH_SHORT).show();
}
```

Toast is a message class. Toast.makeText () is a function that creates a new Toast message. Three parameters are required and the meaning is as follows.
- 1st parameter: Context object - The Context contains the environment and various resources of the App. Since the Activity inherits the Context, you can pass the Activity. 'this' is the MainActivity object, because 'this' corresponds to the current class.
- 2nd parameter: The contents of the string displayed in the Toast message.
- 3rd parameter: The length of time the message is shown. Toast.LENGTH_SHORT is short (almost 3 seconds) and Toast.LENGTH_LONG is long (almost 6 seconds).

The above function returns a Toast object. So we did not use the .show () function on the next line. Instead we combined two functions. Toast.show () is a function that displays the generated message on the screen.

Let's check the results in the emulator. When you run the example, the Toast message appears at the bottom of the screen and disappears after a while.

2) Change the position of Toast message

By default, the Toast message is displayed at the bottom of the screen. You can change the position using the Gravity property. First, delete the contents of the makeQuiz () function as shown below.

```
public void makeQuiz() {

}
```

Then enter the new code as shown below. This is a code that creates a Toast message and positions it up and right.

[Source code copy link : https://goo.gl/KgKZym => Code-5]

```
public void makeQuiz() {
    Toast toast = Toast.makeText(this, "Toast-Gravity", Toast.LENGTH_LONG);
    toast.setGravity(Gravity.TOP | Gravity.RIGHT, 50, 50);
    toast.show();
}
```

Here is the code to create a toast message and store it in a variable named toast.

```
Toast toast = Toast.makeText(this, "Toast-Gravity", Toast.LENGTH_LONG);
```

Below is a code that specifies where the toast message is displayed.

```
toast.setGravity(Gravity.TOP | Gravity.RIGHT, 50, 50);
```

Toast.setGravity () is a function that specifies the location of the toast message. Three parameters are required and their types are as follows.

- 1st parameter: Position of the message. The available attribute values for positioning are as follows and can be specified in duplicate with an or symbol ('|').
= Gravity.LEFT: Left horizontally
= Gravity.CENTER_HORIZONTAL: Horizontal center
= Gravity.RIGHT: Horizontally right
= Gravity.TOP: Vertically upward
= Gravity.CENTER_VERTICAL: Vertically centered
= Gravity.BOTTOM: Vertically downward
- 2nd parameter: Horizontal offset value (horizontal margin)
- 3rd parameter: Vertical offset value (vertical margin)

Let's run the example again and check the results. This time the Toast message is displayed in the upper-right corner of the screen.

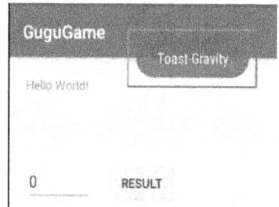

[Exercise] Toast Message
1. Create a new source project and set name to 'ToastEx'.
Make one EditText and one Button widget in the layout file.

2. When user clicks the button, display the string entered in EditText to the Toast message.

3. Specify the location of the Toast message in the center of the screen (both horizontal & vertical).

Java Coding with Android programming 1   Dennis (Donggeun Jung)

N. Multiplication table game

[Key point of this chapter]

Type cast of string
- Change string to integer type : <integer variable> = Integer.parseInt(<string>);
Ex)int num = Integer.parseInt("21");   // num : 21

How to use Toast message
- Create & display Toast message on screen : Toast.makeText(<Context object>, <message string>, <length of time >).show()
Ex) Toast.makeText(this, "This is a Toast message", Toast.LENGTH_SHORT).show();

1) Create multiplication table question

Let's complete a game. Load 'GuguGame' that we made last time. The operation sequence is as follows.
- When the app launches, it will create a multiplication question and display it in TextView,
- The user enters the answer in EditText,
- Press the Result Button to show whether the answer is correct or not.

Let's add a function to create a random number. Make a new function under the makeQuiz () function and enter the following code. It is the same as the random number generation function that we made at last time.

[Source code copy link : https://goo.gl/KgKZym => Code-6]

```java
public int getRandom (int max, int offset) {
    int nResult = (int)(Math.random() * max) + offset;
    return nResult;
}
```

You can use the above function to print out the multiplication problem in TextView. First, delete the contents of the makeQuiz () function as shown below.

```java
public void makeQuiz() {

}
```

Then enter the new code as shown below. This is the code that creates the text of multiplication question and displays it in the TextView.

[Source code copy link : https://goo.gl/KgKZym => Code-7]

```java
public void makeQuiz() {
```

```
        int left = getRandom (8, 2);
        int right = getRandom (8, 2);
        textView1.setText(left + " * " + right + " = ?");
        nResult = left * right;
    }
```

Below is a code that creates two random numbers between 2 and 9, and stores them in two int variables. When creating a random number, the range is 8, and the minimum value is 2. This will create a random number between the minimum value of 2 and the maximum value of 9.

```
        int left = getRandom (7, 2);
        int right = getRandom (7, 2);
```

Below is the code that creates a string question and displays it in the TextView. We added a '*' mark between the two numbers, and appended '=?' to the right end. For example, if two random numbers are 5 and 8, the string "5 * 8 =?" is created.

```
        textView1.setText(left + " * " + right + " = ?");
```

Below is the code that stores the multiplication result into member variables. This is to determine whether the value user entered is correct or not.

```
        nResult = left * right;
```

Let's run the source project. Multiplication question is displayed.

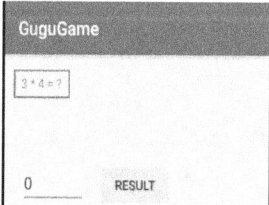

2) Judging the correct answer

Let's make a function that determines if the user enters a number in the EditText is the right answer. Make a new function under the getRandom () function and add the code below. onBtnResult () is an event function that executes when the user presses the Button.

[Source code copy link : https://goo.gl/KgKZym => Code-8]

```
public void onBtnResult(View v) {
```

```
        String strAnswer = editText1.getText().toString();
        int answer = Integer.parseInt(strAnswer);
        if( answer == nResult )
            Toast.makeText(this, nResult + " – Correct answer!",
            Toast.LENGTH_LONG).show();
        else
            Toast.makeText(this, "Wrong answer - " + nResult,
                Toast.LENGTH_LONG).show();
        makeQuiz();
    }
```

Below is the code that gets the string entered in EditText and changes it to a number.

```
        String strAnswer = editText1.getText().toString();
        int answer = Integer.parseInt(strAnswer);
```

Below is the code that outputs the string "Correct Answers" as a toast message when user entered the correct answer, and the string "Wrong answer" as a toast message when user entered the wrong answer.

```
        if( answer == nResult )
            Toast.makeText(this, nResult + " – Correct answer!",
                Toast.LENGTH_LONG).show();
        else
            Toast.makeText(this, "Wrong answer - " + nResult,
                Toast.LENGTH_LONG).show();
```

The last line below calls a function that displays a new multiplication question in the TextView. If user solve one question, computer will continue to make new question.

```
        makeQuiz();
```

We finished making multiplication game. Run the example and enter the correct answer in EditText and press the Button. Toast message tells you whether the answer is correct or not. And a new question appears.

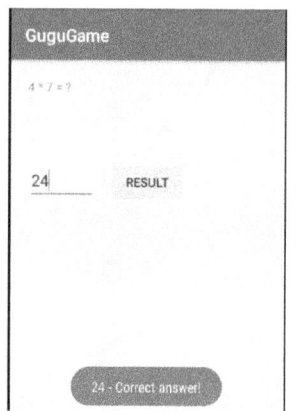 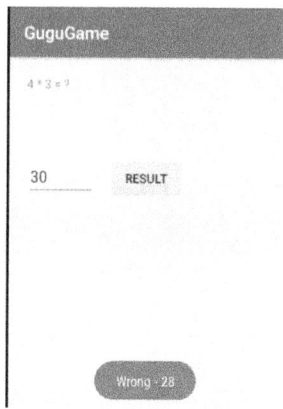

The game example is completed. The complete code for this example is shown below. Thank you.

```java
package com.example.gugugame;
import android.support.v7.app.AppCompatActivity;
import android.os.Bundle;
import android.view.Gravity;
import android.view.View;
import android.widget.EditText;
import android.widget.TextView;
import android.widget.Toast;

public class MainActivity extends AppCompatActivity {
    TextView textView1;
    EditText editText1;
    int nResult;

    @Override
    protected void onCreate(Bundle savedInstanceState) {
        super.onCreate(savedInstanceState);
        setContentView(R.layout.activity_main);
        textView1 = (TextView)findViewById(R.id.textView1);
        editText1 = (EditText)findViewById(R.id.editText1);
        makeQuiz();
    }

    public void makeQuiz() {
```

```java
        int left = getRandom (8, 2);
        int right = getRandom (8, 2);
        textView1.setText(left + " * " + right + " = ?");
        nResult = left * right;
    }

    public int getRandom (int max, int offset) {
        int nResult = (int)(Math.random() * max) + offset;
        return nResult;
    }

    public void onBtnResult(View v) {
        String strAnswer = editText1.getText().toString();
        int answer = Integer.parseInt(strAnswer);
        if( answer == nResult )
            Toast.makeText(this, nResult + " - Correct answer!", Toast.LENGTH_LONG).show();
        else
            Toast.makeText(this, "Wrong - " + nResult, Toast.LENGTH_LONG).show();
        makeQuiz();
    }
}
```

[Exercise] Making mathematics game
1. Create a new source project and set name to 'MathPang'.
Create a TextView, EditTex, and Button widget in the layout file.

2. Run the example to display the numeric calculation problem in the TextView.
Create a formula by placing a multiplication sign (*) or a addition sign (+) between two numbers between 2 and 9 generated by a random number.
   ex) 3 * 5 = ? or 9 + 7 = ?

3. If the user enters an answer in the EditText and clicks the button, the Toast message will indicate whether the answer is correct or not.

4. When user solves the problem, automatically display the new question in the TextView.

[Exercise] Modify create random function
Below is creating random number function's source code. The parameters are range and min value
Modify function to receive two parameters which are max and min value.

```java
public int getRandom (int max, int offset) {
    int nResult = (int)(Math.random() * max) + offset;
    return nResult;
}
```

O. switch-case conditional statement

This time, we will make a number up and down game. The computer makes a random number between 1 and 100, and user matchs them. If the correct answer is bigger than the number entered by the user, the word 'Up' is displayed. If it is smaller, the word 'Down' is displayed. When user input the correct answer, the word 'correct' is displayed.

There are two Buttons. You must use conditional statements to determine which of the two buttons user selected, when user pressed the Button. The switch - case statement is more useful than if - else statement when determining which of the various numbers.

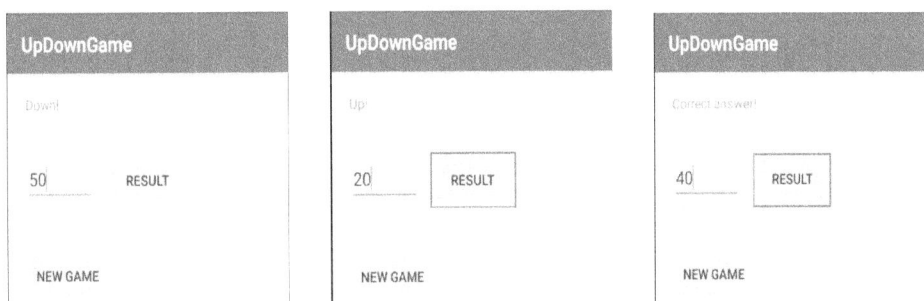

[Key point of this chapter]

```
# How to use switch case conditional statement #
- regular switch case conditional statement format
switch( <integer> ) {
    case <compareing value 1> :
        <code runned when integer == compareing value 1>
        break;
case <compareing value 2> :
        <code runned when integer == compareing value 2>
        break;
default :
        <code runned when integer != compareing value 1 && integer != compareing value 2>
        break;
}
Ex)
int num = 2;
switch( num ) {
    case 1 :         // determine num is equal to 1
        textView1.setText("num == 1");    // this code is not runned
        break;       // if break is runned, computer escape from switch-case conditional statement
```

```
case 2 :         // determine num is equal to 2
      textView1.setText("num == 2");     // this code is runned
      break;         // if omit break, the next code will be runned
  default :         // integer is neither 1 nor 2
      textView1.setText("num != 1 && num != 2");     // this code is not runned
      break;
}
```

1) Generate Random number

(1) Creating new source project
Create a new source project. Set name the project 'UpDownGame'.

(2) Making widgets in Layout file
Let's add a widget to the screen. Go to the layout information file (activity_main.xml) and change the properties of the automatically generated TextView as shown below.
⟨TextView⟩
- id : textView1

We will make one EditText and two Button widgets below it. EditText can be found by selecting 'Plain Text' in the 'Text Fields' group.

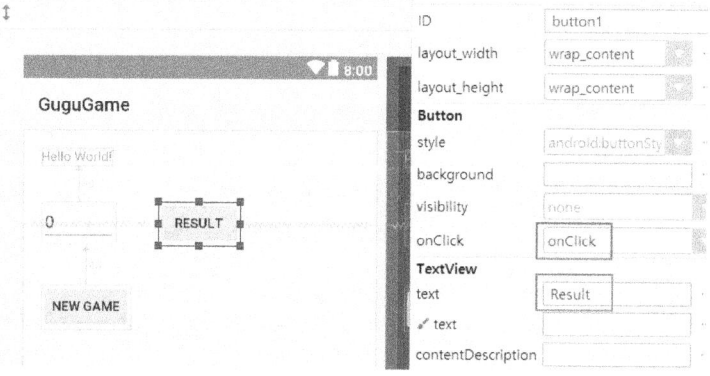

Change the properties of each widget as shown below.

⟨ EditText ⟩
- layout:width : 80dp
- id : editText1
- text : 0

⟨ 1st Button ⟩
- id : button1

- onClick : onClick
- text : Result

〈 2nd Button 〉
- id : button2
- onClick : onClick
- text : New game

We added two buttons. Did not you feel something strange? The onClick property specifies the name of the click event function, and two buttons have the same function name.
'Then computer will not know which button was pressed when the event function was executed ... '
If you think about it, you can think that you are studying properly. Which button the user has selected can be determined by the ID value. The ID of the first button is specified as button1, and the second button is specified as button2. We specified ID as a string, but internally it is stored as a numeric value. For example, the ID button1 has 101 internally, and button2 has 102.
You can use if - else conditional statement to compare numeric values, but switch - case conditional statement is more convenient. After a while, we will learn how to use it through practice.

You can also copy the layout information codes. Press the Text button to the right of the Design button at the bottom of the screen and go to text editing mode. When the layout text editing mode appears, delete all the contents and enter the following code.

[Source code copy link : https://goo.gl/h49k2v => Code-1]

```xml
<?xml version="1.0" encoding="utf-8"?>
<RelativeLayout xmlns:android="http://schemas.android.com/apk/res/android"
    xmlns:tools="http://schemas.android.com/tools"
    android:layout_width="match_parent"
    android:layout_height="match_parent"
    android:padding="20dp">

    <TextView
        android:layout_width="wrap_content"
        android:layout_height="wrap_content"
        android:text="Hello World!"
        android:id="@+id/textView1" />

    <EditText
        android:layout_width="80dp"
        android:layout_height="wrap_content"
```

```
            android:id="@+id/editText1"
            android:layout_below="@+id/textView1"
            android:layout_alignParentStart="true"
            android:layout_marginTop="39dp"
            android:text="0" />


    <Button
            android:layout_width="wrap_content"
            android:layout_height="wrap_content"
            android:text="Result"
            android:id="@+id/button1"
            android:layout_alignTop="@+id/editText1"
            android:layout_centerHorizontal="true"
            android:onClick="onClick" />


    <Button
            android:layout_width="wrap_content"
            android:layout_height="wrap_content"
            android:text="New game"
            android:id="@+id/button2"
            android:layout_below="@+id/button1"
            android:layout_marginTop="43dp"
            android:onClick="onClick" />
</RelativeLayout>
```

(3) Initialize widgets by source code
We will declare the widgets as member variables to display the message in the TextView. Go to the activity source file (MainActivity.java) and add the following new code below the beginning of the class. If a red letter is displayed, press the shortcut key Alt + Enter.

[Source code copy link : https://goo.gl/h49k2v => Code-2]

```
public class MainActivity extends AppCompatActivity {
    TextView textView1;
    EditText editText1;
    int nResult;
```

We have declared one TextView, one EditText, and one int as member variables. nResult will store a random number.

We will save the widget to the above variable. Add the following new code to the end of onCreate () function.

[Source code copy link : https://goo.gl/h49k2v => Code-3]

```java
protected void onCreate(Bundle savedInstanceState) {
    super.onCreate(savedInstanceState);
    setContentView(R.layout.activity_main);
    textView1 = (TextView)findViewById(R.id.textView1);
    editText1 = (EditText)findViewById(R.id.editText1);
    makeQuiz();
}
```

TextView and EditText widget objects are stored in member variables. And the code ran a function named makeQuiz (). This function has not yet been created, it will create a random number between 1 and 100, and store it in the nResult variable.

Create two new functions under the onCreate () function and enter the new code as shown below. If a red letter is displayed, press the shortcut key Alt + Enter.

[Source code copy link : https://goo.gl/h49k2v => Code-4]

```java
public void makeQuiz() {
    nResult = getRandom (100, 1);
    textView1.setText("Try a number between 1 and 100.");
}

public int getRandom (int max, int offset) {
    int nResult = (int)(Math.random() * max) + offset;
    return nResult;
}
```

getRandom () is a function that creates a random number. The code specified a range of 100 and a minimum of 1. This will create a random number between 1 and 100.

```java
nResult = getRandom (100, 1);
```

Let's run the example. When the app is launched, the TextView will display the string 'Try a number between 1 and 100'.

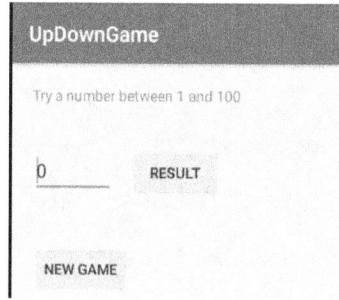

2) switch case conditional statement

Let's implement the function to determine whether Up, Down or Correct answer, when the user enters a number in EditText and presses the 'Result' button. To do this, you need to know which of the two buttons user has selected. Create a new function under the getRandom () function, name it onClick (), and enter the code as shown below. If you see a red letter, press the shortcut key Alt + Enter.

[Source code copy link : https://goo.gl/h49k2v => Code-5]

```java
public void onClick(View v) {
    int id = v.getId();
    switch( id ) {
        case R.id.button1 :
            textView1.setText("Button-1");
            break;
        case R.id.button2 :
            textView1.setText("Button-2");
            break;
    }
}
```

Below is the code that gets the ID of the button the user clicked, and stores it in an integer variable. The button widget is passed as a parameter when the onClick () function is executed. View.getId () is a function that returns the ID of the widget. View class is all widget's super class. Therefore Button object can be changed to View type.

```java
int id = v.getId();
```

Let's look at how to use the switch case conditional statement. In the example below, if the value of A is equal to B, the code C is executed. If the value of A is equal to D, code E is executed. If A is neither B nor D, then F is executed.

```
switch ( A ) {
    case B :
        C ;
        break;
    case D :
        E ;
        break;
    default :
        F ;
        break;
}
```

The case statement needs a break statement at the end. break means to escape a conditional statement or loop statement. In this case, when break is executed, computer escapes the switch statement and the next code is not executed. Therefore, if there is no break at the end of the case statement, then the next case statement is executed.

The parentheses of switch () syntax can only contain integer number (int, long, short, byte), character (char), and string (String). Real number is not allowed.
The comparison value of the case statement is also numeric only and is not suitable for comparing which value is bigger or smaller.

In the code below, R.id.button1 is the ID of the first button. This looks like a string, but internally it is recognized as a number because the system stores the number in a variable named button1.
When the user presses the first button, the character 'Button-1' is output to the TextView.

```
case R.id.button1 :
    textView1.setText("Button-1");
```

The next code will output the text 'Button-2' to the TextView when the user presses the second button.

Run the example and press the two buttons alternately. If you see another character in the TextView each time you press the button, the app is working correctly.

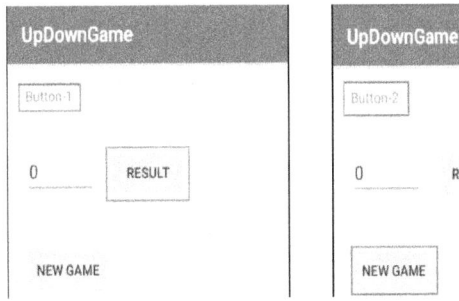

[Exercise] switch case conditional statement
1. Create a new source project and set name to 'AlphabetNumber'.
Make one TextView, one EditTex, and one Button widget in the layout file.

2. If the user enters a number between 1 and 4 in the EditText and clicks the button, convert it to Alphabet and output it to TextView.
ex) If user entered 1, print 'one'. If user entered 2, print 'two'.
   If user entered 3, print 'three'. If user entered 4, print 'four'.
  Implement by using switch - case conditional statements instead of if - else conditional statements.

P. Number up & down game

[Key point of this chapter]

```
# How to use if – else #
- if else if conditional statement :
if ( <conditional statement 1> ) {
<source code runned when conditional statement 1 is true code>
} else if ( <conditional statement 2> ) {
<source code runned when conditional statement 2 is true code>
} else {
<source code runned when conditional statement 1 & 2 are both false>
}
Ex)
if( 3 == 1 ) {          // conditional statement-1
     textView1.setText("3 and 1 is equal");    // runned when conditional statement 1 is true
} else if( 3 < 1 ) {    // conditional statement-2
textView1.setText("3 is smaller than 1");     // runned when conditional statement 2 is true
} else {
textView1.setText("3 is bigger than 1");      // runned when conditional statement 1 && 2 are both false
}
```

1) Implement 'Result' Button's functionality

Pressing the 'Result' button will get the number entered in EditText to determine if it is Up, Down, or the correct answer. First, remove the unnecessary code from the onClick () function as shown below.

```java
public void onClick(View v) {
    int id = v.getId();
    switch( id ) {
        case R.id.button1 :


            break;
        case R.id.button2 :


            break;
    }
}
```

Then enter the new code as shown below. We entered the if - else conditional statement in the switch - case conditional statement. The switch - case is more convenient when comparing one value with others one by one, and if - else is more convenient when determine which is bigger.

[Source code copy link : https:// goo.gl/h49k2v => Code-6]

```java
public void onClick(View v) {
    int id = v.getId();
    switch( id ) {
        case R.id.button1 :
            String strAnswer = editText1.getText().toString();
            int answer = Integer.parseInt(strAnswer);
            if( nResult == answer )
                textView1.setText("Correct answer!");
            else if( nResult > answer )
                textView1.setText("Up!");
            else
                textView1.setText("Down!");
            break;
        case R.id.button2 :

            break;
    }
}
```

Here's the code that gets the user-entered string in EditText and changes it to an integer.

```java
String strAnswer = editText1.getText().toString();
int answer = Integer.parseInt(strAnswer);
```

Below is a code that displays the text "Correct answer!" in the TextView, if the random number and the value entered by the user are the same.

```java
if( nResult == answer )
    textView1.setText("Correct answer!");
```

Below is a code that displays the word 'Up' in the TextView, if the random number is bigger than the value entered by the user.

```
else if( nResult > answer )
    textView1.setText("Up!");
```

Below is a code that displays the word 'Down' in the TextView, if the random number is less than the value entered by the user. The random number is less than user input value, because it is not bigger and not equal neither.

```
else
    textView1.setText("Down!");
```

Let's run the example and check the results. Enter any number between 1 and 100 in EditText and press the 'Result' button. If 'Up' is displayed, enter a bigger number and press the 'Result' button. If 'Down' is displayed, enter a smaller number and press the 'Result' button. Continue until 'Correct answer!' is displayed.

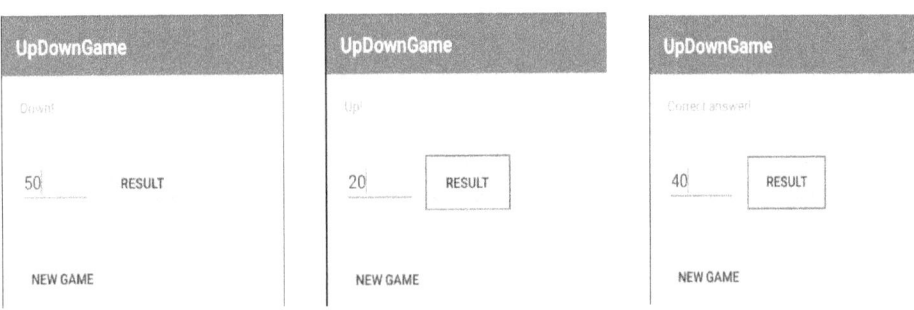

2) Implement 'New game' Button's functionality

Finally, let's make the 'New game' Button's functionality to create a new random number and start a new game. In the second case statement of the onClick() function, add the following new code.

[Source code copy link : https://goo.gl/h49k2v => Code-7]

```java
public void onClick(View v) {
    int id = v.getId();
    switch( id ) {
        case R.id.button1 :
            ~
            break;
        case R.id.button2 :
            makeQuiz();
            break;
    }
}
```

Pressing the second button calls the function to start a new game. Let's run the example and guess the number which computer selected. Press the 'New game' button when you entered the correct answer. TextView will display the text 'Try a number between 1 and 100'. A new game has begun.

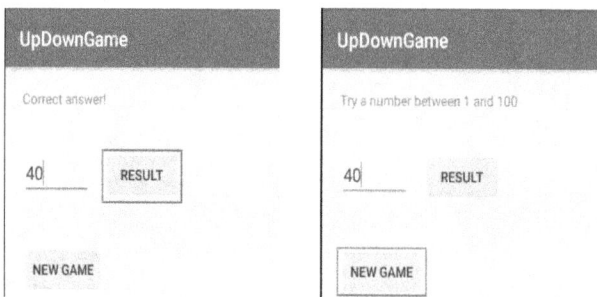

The Up and Down game example is completed. The complete code for this example is shown below.

```java
public class MainActivity extends AppCompatActivity {
    TextView textView1;
    EditText editText1;
    int nResult;

    @Override
    protected void onCreate(Bundle savedInstanceState) {
        super.onCreate(savedInstanceState);
        setContentView(R.layout.activity_main);
        textView1 = (TextView)findViewById(R.id.textView1);
        editText1 = (EditText)findViewById(R.id.editText1);
        makeQuiz();
    }

    public void makeQuiz() {
        nResult = getRandom (100, 1);
        textView1.setText("Try a number between 1 and 100.");
    }

    public int getRandom (int max, int offset) {
        int nResult = (int)(Math.random() * max) + offset;
        return nResult;
```

```java
    }

    public void onClick(View v) {
        int id = v.getId();
        switch( id ) {
            case R.id.button1 :
                String strAnswer = editText1.getText().toString();
                int answer = Integer.parseInt(strAnswer);
                if( nResult == answer )
                    textView1.setText("Correct answer!");
                else if( nResult > answer )
                    textView1.setText("Up!");
                else
                    textView1.setText("Down!");
                break;
            case R.id.button2 :
                makeQuiz();
                break;
        }
    }
}
```

[Exercise] Increase number by 1 or 2
1. Create a new source project and set name to 'Add1or2'.
Create one TextView and two Button widgets in the layout file.

2. Set the caption text of the TextView is 0,
   Set the caption text of the first Button is 1,
   Set the caption text of the second Button to 2.
   Specify the click event function of the two Buttons as both 'onClick'.

3. Implement a function that increases the number of TextView when the user clicks the button.
   If user click 1st button, it increases by 1,
   If user click 2nd button, it increases by 2.

Q. Rock, Paper, Scissors game & complex operator

This time we will make a game of rock-paper-scissors. Computer will select one of the three types of rock-paper-scissors, and when the user presses one of the three buttons, a toast message will be displayed indicating who won.

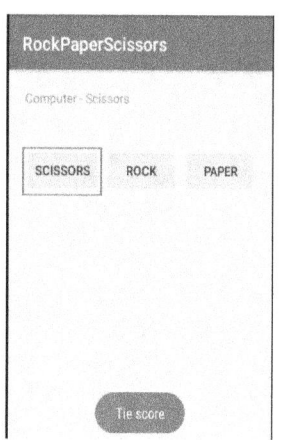 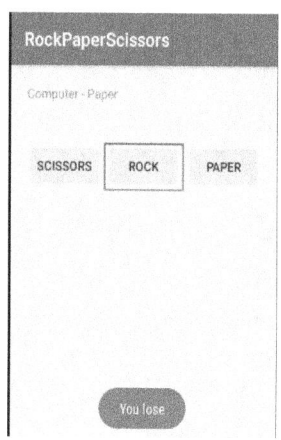 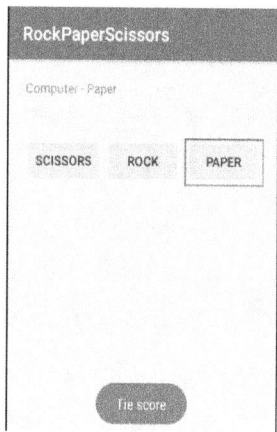

[Key point of this chapter]

```
# How to use random number #
- Create & return random number function definition
public int getRandom (int max, int offset) {      // max : range of random number, offset : minimum value of random number
   int nResult = (int)(Math.random() * max) + offset;    // create random number
       return nResult;       // sending of random number
}
- Use of creating random number function
int random = getRandom(3, 1);     // random : one of 1, 2 or 3
```

1) Select rock, paper, scissors by Random number

(1) Create new source project
Create a new source project. Select main menu [File 〉 New 〉 New Project…]. Set name of the project to 'RockPaperScissors'.

(2) Make widgets in Layout file
Let's add a widget to the screen. Go to the layout information file (activity_main.xml) and change the properties of the automatically generated TextView as shown below.

〈TextView〉
- id : textView1
- text : Choose one of the Rock, Paper, Scissors

And create three Button widgets below it.

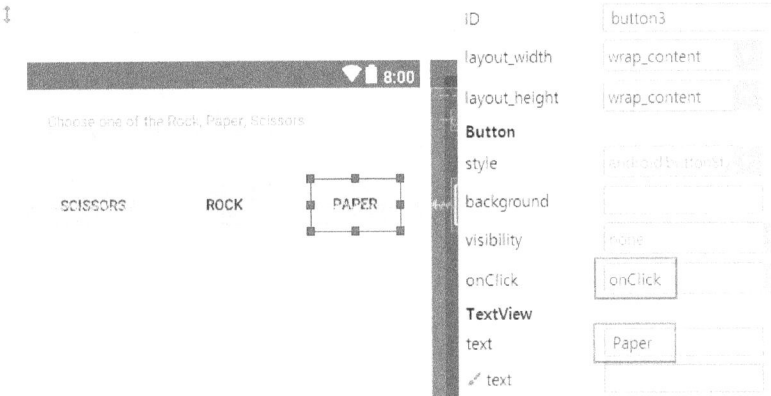

You can change the properties of each widget as shown below.

〈 1st Button 〉
- id : button1
- onClick : onClick
- text : Scissors

〈 2nd Button 〉
- id : button2
- onClick : onClick
- text : Rock

〈 3rd Button 〉
- id : button3
- onClick : onClick
text : Paper

After adding all the buttons, it is recommended to drag the 3rd button with the mouse and attach it to the right end. The second button is good for move to the center in the horizontal direction.

You can also copy the layout information. Press the Text button to the right of the Design button at the bottom of the screen and go to text editing mode. When the layout text editing mode appears, delete all the contents and enter the following code.

[Source code copy link : https://goo.gl/3Gj8e5 => Code-1]

```
<?xml version="1.0" encoding="utf-8"?>
```

```xml
<RelativeLayout xmlns:android="http://schemas.android.com/apk/res/android"
    xmlns:tools="http://schemas.android.com/tools"
    android:layout_width="match_parent"
    android:layout_height="match_parent"
    android:padding="20dp"
    tools:context="com.example.rockpaperscissors.MainActivity">

    <TextView
        android:layout_width="wrap_content"
        android:layout_height="wrap_content"
        android:text="Choose one of the Rock, Paper, Scissors"
        android:id="@+id/textView1" />

    <Button
        android:layout_width="wrap_content"
        android:layout_height="wrap_content"
        android:text="Scissors"
        android:id="@+id/button1"
        android:layout_below="@+id/textView1"
        android:layout_alignParentStart="true"
        android:layout_marginTop="44dp"
        android:onClick="onClick" />

    <Button
        android:layout_width="wrap_content"
        android:layout_height="wrap_content"
        android:text="Rock"
        android:id="@+id/button2"
        android:layout_alignTop="@+id/button1"
        android:layout_centerHorizontal="true"
        android:onClick="onClick" />

    <Button
        android:layout_width="wrap_content"
```

```
            android:layout_height="wrap_content"
            android:text="Paper"
            android:id="@+id/button3"
            android:onClick="onClick"
            android:layout_alignTop="@+id/button2"
            android:layout_alignParentEnd="true" />
  </RelativeLayout>
```

(3) Initialize widgets by source code
We will declare the widget as a member variable to display the message in the TextView. Go to the activity source file (MainActivity.java) and add the following new code below the beginning of the class. If a red letter is displayed, press the shortcut key Alt + Enter.

[Source code copy link : https://goo.gl/3Gj8e5 => Code-2]

```java
public class MainActivity extends AppCompatActivity {
    TextView textView1;
    int nResult;
```

We have declared one TextView and one int as member variables. In int variable we will store the rock-paper-scissors value.

We will save the widget to the above variable. Add the following new code to the end of onCreate () function.

[Source code copy link : https://goo.gl/3Gj8e5 => Code-3]

```java
protected void onCreate(Bundle savedInstanceState) {
    super.onCreate(savedInstanceState);
    setContentView(R.layout.activity_main);
    textView1 = (TextView)findViewById(R.id.textView1);
    makeQuiz();
}
```

TextView has been saved to a member variable. And the code ran a function named makeQuiz (). This function has not yet been created, it will make a random number between 0 and 2, and store it in the nResult variable.

Make two new functions under the onCreate () function and enter the new code as shown below. If a red letter is displayed, press the shortcut key Alt + Enter.

[Source code copy link : https://goo.gl/3Gj8e5 => Code-4]

```java
public void makeQuiz() {
```

```
        nResult = getRandom (3, 0);
    }


    public int getRandom (int max, int offset) {
        int nResult = (int)(Math.random() * max) + offset;
        return nResult;
    }
```

getRandom () is a function that creates a random number. Below is a code that generates a random number corresponding to one of rock-paper-scissors. We have specified a range of 3, and a minimum of 0. 0 means scissors, 1 means rock, and 2 means beam.

```
        nResult = getRandom (3, 0);
```

2) Determine the winner of game

(1) Display the computer selection on the screen
When the user presses a Button, the computer will convert the selected random number to a string and display it in the TextView. Add a new function below the getRandom () function and enter the code below. This is Button click event function.

[Source code copy link : https://goo.gl/3Gj8e5 => Code-5]

```
public void onClick(View v) {
    switch( nResult ) {
        case 0 :
            textView1.setText("Computer - Scissors");
            break;
        case 1 :
            textView1.setText("Computer - Rock");
            break;
        default :
            textView1.setText("Computer - Paper");
            break;
    }
}
```

If the random number is 0, 'Computer - Scissors' is displayed, if 1 'Computer - Rock' is displayed, if 2 'Comput er - Paper' is displayed in the TextView.

Run the example and press a button. TextView displays one of the rock-paper-scissors selected by the computer.

(2) Change users selection to number

Let's change the button selection by the user to a number. If user chose 'scissors', it will be changed to 0, if 'rock' it will be changed to '1', or if 'paper' it will be changed to 2. This is also handy if you use the switch case statement. There is another way to use an array, but since we have not yet learned the array, we will try it next time. Add new code to the end of the onClick () function as shown below.

[Source code copy link : https://goo.gl/3Gj8e5 => Code-6]

```java
public void onClick(View v) {
    switch( nResult ) {
        ~
    }

    int userSel = 2;
    switch( v.getId() ) {
        case R.id.button1 :
            userSel = 0;
            break;
        case R.id.button2 :
            userSel = 1;
            break;
    }
}
```

The following declares an integer variable userSel and initializes it to 2. This means the variable is initialized to 'Paper'.

```
int userSel = 2;
```

Below is the code that compares the ID of the button user selected with the switch statement.

```
switch( v.getId() ) {
```

Below code stores 0 in the userSel variable when the ID of the button is button1. This code is executed when user selected the 'Scissors' button.

```
case R.id.button1 :
    userSel = 0;
```

Below code stores 1 in the userSel variable when the ID of the button is button2. This code is executed when user selected the 'Rock' button.

```
case R.id.button2 :
    userSel = 1;
```

When 'Paper' is selected, no further processing is performed. Since we initialized the userSel variable to 2 at first, it is automatically 'Paper' when it is neither 'scissors' nor 'rocks'.

(3) Determine the winner of game
Now that you have changed the button user selected to a number. Computer can now determine who has won the game. Rather than simply comparing the size of the numbers, you should apply the rule such as rocks beat scissors. The number of cases that can appear is all nine, and can be broadly divided into the following groups.

First, if computers and user have the same number, that means tie score.
Second, in the following cases, the user has won.
- People: 1 (Rock) & Computer: 0 (Scissors)
- Person: 2 (Paper) & Computer: 1 (Rock)
- Person: 0 (Scissors) & Computer: 2 (Paper)
Except for the case above, user lost.

We will implement a function that determines whether the user has won or lost, and displays the result in a Toast message. Enter the new code below at the bottom of the onClick () function.

[Source code copy link : https://goo.gl/3Gj8e5 => Code-7]

```
public void onClick(View v) {
    switch( nResult ) {
        ~
    }
    int userSel = 2;
    switch( v.getId() ) {
```

```
        ~
    }

    if( userSel == nResult ) {
        Toast.makeText(this, "Tie score", Toast.LENGTH_SHORT).show();
        makeQuiz();
        return;
    }
    boolean win = false;
    if( (userSel > nResult) && (userSel - nResult == 1) )
        win = true;
    else if( userSel == 0 && nResult == 2 )
        win = true;


    if( win )
        Toast.makeText(this, "You win", Toast.LENGTH_SHORT).show();
    else
        Toast.makeText(this, "You lose", Toast.LENGTH_SHORT).show();
}
```

Below is a code that displays the word 'Tie score' in a Toast message, when a person and computer have chosen the same type.
return is a command to escape the function. If in case tie score, there is no need to execute the rest code. To start a new game, call the makeQuiz () function.

```
    if( userSel == nResult ) {
        Toast.makeText(this, "Tie score", Toast.LENGTH_SHORT).show();
        makeQuiz();
        return;
```

The following declares a boolean variable and initializes it to false. If the value of this variable is true, the user has won, and if it is false the user lost.
If the value selected by the user is one bigger than the value selected by the computer, change the win variable to true because the person has won.

```
        boolean win = false;
        if( userSel - nResult == 1 )
```

```
win = true;
```

Below is store true to the win variable, if the person is 0 (scissors) and the computer is 2 (paper). The && symbol is true when both left and right are true. The && symbol is true only when userSel is 0, nResult is 2, and the && symbol is false even though only one of the two conditions is false.

```
else if( userSel == 0 && nResult == 2 )
    win = true;
```

'&&' is a compound operator and reads 'And'. The whole statement is true only if both the left and right conditionals are true.

Among the frequently used compound operators, there is '||' and read 'Or'. If only one of the left and right conditional statements is true, then the whole statement is true. Only if both are false is the whole false.

The result of if - else conditional statement is the same as the following. You can combine two conditionals together using the '||' symbol.

```
if( (userSel - nResult == 1) || ( userSel == 0 && nResult == 2 ) )
    win = true;
```

Below is a code that displays the word 'You win' in a Toast message when the user wins, and 'You lose' when user lost.

```
if( win )
    Toast.makeText(this, "You win", Toast.LENGTH_SHORT).show();
else
    Toast.makeText(this, "You lose", Toast.LENGTH_SHORT).show();
```

Run the example and press one of the scissors-rock-paper Buttons. The type selected by the computer is displayed in the TextView, and the results appear in the Toast message at the bottom of the screen.

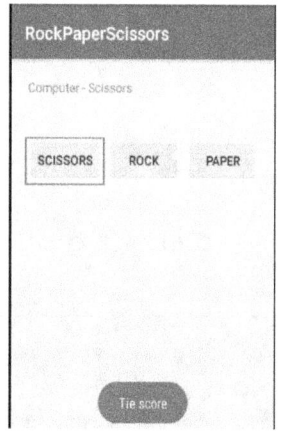

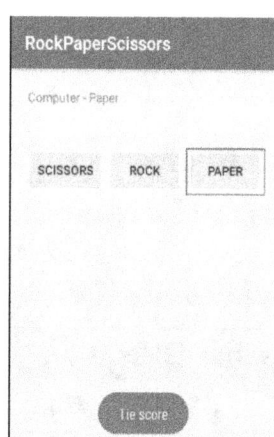

(4) Start a new game automatically

We will update the Button's functionality to display the results and automatically start a new game. You can add the makeQuiz () function to the onClick () function as shown below.

[Source code copy link : https://goo.gl/3Gj8e5 => Code-8]

```java
public void onClick(View v) {
    ~
    if( win )
        Toast.makeText(this, "You win", Toast.LENGTH_SHORT).show();
    else
        Toast.makeText(this, "You lose", Toast.LENGTH_SHORT).show();
    makeQuiz();
}
```

Run the example again and keep pressing the button. You can now play the rock-paper-scissors game constantly.

Rock-Paper-Scissors game example is completed. The complete code for this example is shown below. Thank you.

```java
public class MainActivity extends AppCompatActivity {
    TextView textView1;
    int nResult;

    @Override
    protected void onCreate(Bundle savedInstanceState) {
        super.onCreate(savedInstanceState);
        setContentView(R.layout.activity_main);
        textView1 = (TextView)findViewById(R.id.textView1);
        makeQuiz();
    }

    public void makeQuiz() {
        nResult = getRandom (3, 0);
    }
```

```java
public int getRandom (int max, int offset) {
    int nResult = (int)(Math.random() * max) + offset;
    return nResult;
}


public void onClick(View v) {
    switch( nResult ) {
        case 0 :
            textView1.setText("Computer - Scissors");
            break;
        case 1 :
            textView1.setText("Computer - Rock");
            break;
        default :
            textView1.setText("Computer - Paper");
            break;
    }

    int userSel = 2;
    switch( v.getId() ) {
        case R.id.button1 :
            userSel = 0;
            break;
        case R.id.button2 :
            userSel = 1;
            break;
    }

    if( userSel == nResult ) {
        Toast.makeText(this, "Tie score", Toast.LENGTH_SHORT).show();
        makeQuiz();
        return;
    }
    boolean win = false;
```

```
        if( (userSel > nResult) && (userSel - nResult == 1) )
            win = true;
        else if( userSel == 0 && nResult == 2 )
            win = true;


        if( win )
            Toast.makeText(this, "You win", Toast.LENGTH_SHORT).show();
        else
            Toast.makeText(this, "You lose", Toast.LENGTH_SHORT).show();
        makeQuiz();
    }
}
```

[Exercise] Determin Even

1. Create a new source project and set name to 'DeterminEven'. Make a TextView, two EditTexts, and a Button widget in the layout file.

2. When the user enters two numbers in two EditTexts and presses the Button,
Determine whether the number entered in the first EditText is even or odd.
If the number is even, display 'Even' in the TextView. If the number is odd, display 'Odd' in the TextView.

3. If both numbers are even, display the text "Both are even" in the TextView,
Otherwise, display "Please re-enter." In the TextView.

R. Installing Application to Smart Phone

Let's install the app we created on the actual phone. You can take out your phone at any time, play your own game, and enjoy it with friends and people around you.

[Key point of this chapter]

The sequence of installing application into smartphone
- Enable 'developer option' in phone's Settings
- Enable 'debug mode' in phone's Settings
- Set permission of installing unknown app
- Connect PC and phone by using USB
- Installing application by using Android Studio

1) Enable smartphone debug mode

To install a source project (application) on your smartphone, you need to enable 'debug mode' in settings. To do so, let's check first to see if there is a developer option.
- Go to the Settings in your smartphone.
- If you do not have 'Developer Options' in the System (or General) group, do the following:
- Go to [System > Device information] (or About phone > Software information) and touch 'Build number' 7 times.

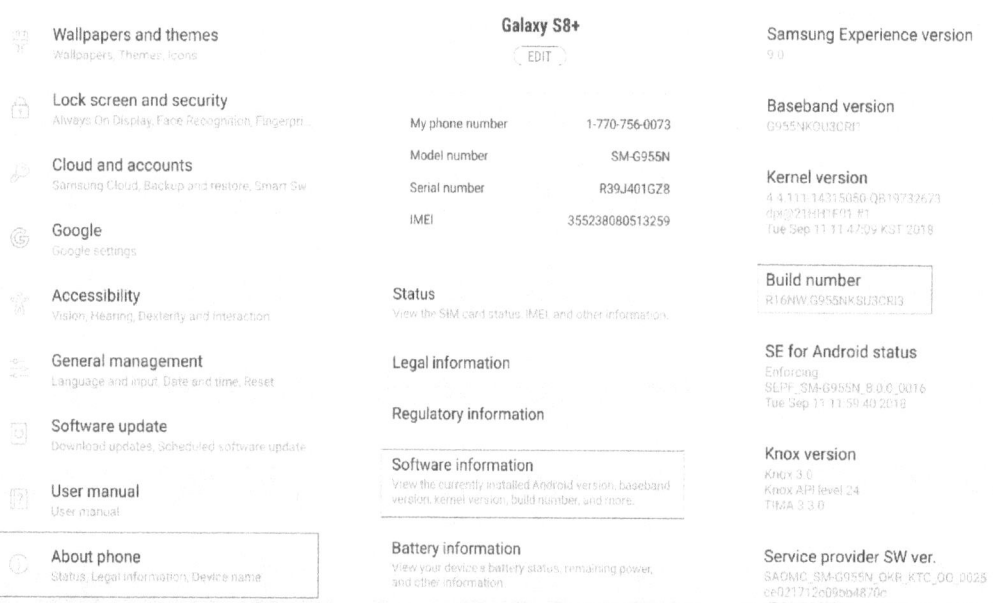

Escape 'Settings' and run again, 'Developer options' item is added (in System group)
- Touch 'Developer options'
- Set on to right-top flipswitch
- Set check 'USB debugging'

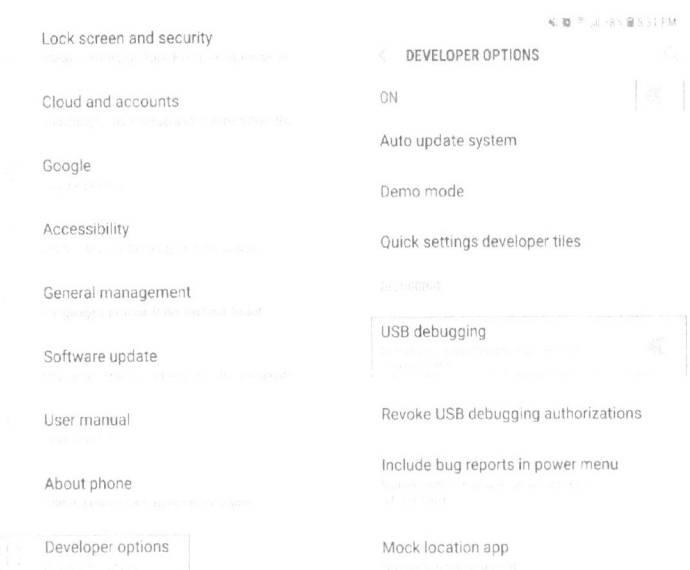

Next you have to give permission to install unknown apps. To allow app installs to phone, follow this steps:
- Navigate to [Settings > Security].
- Check the option 'Unknown sources'.
- Select 'OK' or 'Trust' on the popup message.

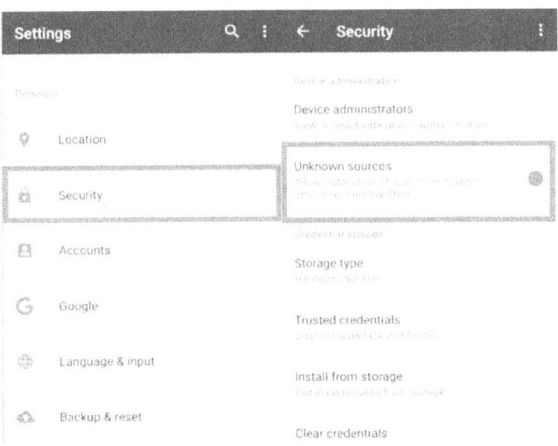

2) Connect PC and smartphone by USB cable
- Connect PC and smart phone by cable.
- If 'Allow access to phone data?' popup dialog is shown press 'ALLOW' button.
- If 'Allow USB debugging?' popup dialog is shown, check 'Always allow from this computer' and press 'OK' button.

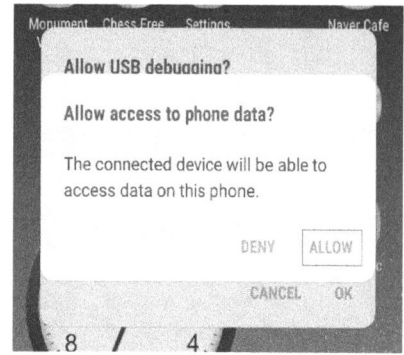

Let's install a source project to smart phone.
- Run Android studio and load previous source project.
- Press 'Run' button in toolbar.
- When 'Select Deployment Target' popup dialog is shown, select hardware device in list. Set check 'Use same device for future launches' and click 'OK' button.

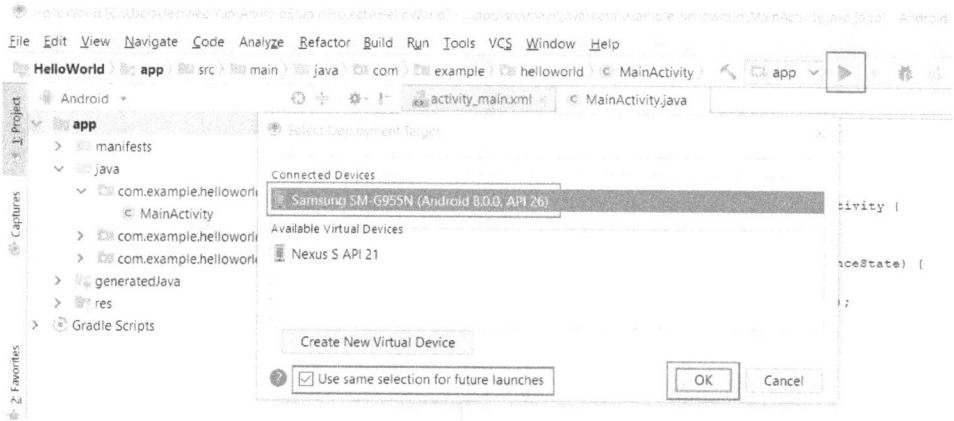

- If 'Instant Run' popup dialog is shown, click 'Install and Continue' button. Wait until install is finished.

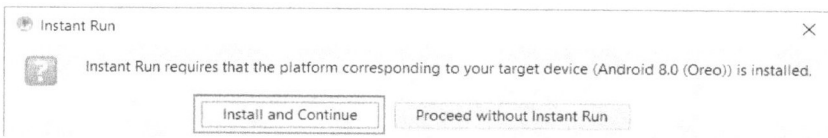

- When installing is finished, press 'Finish' button.

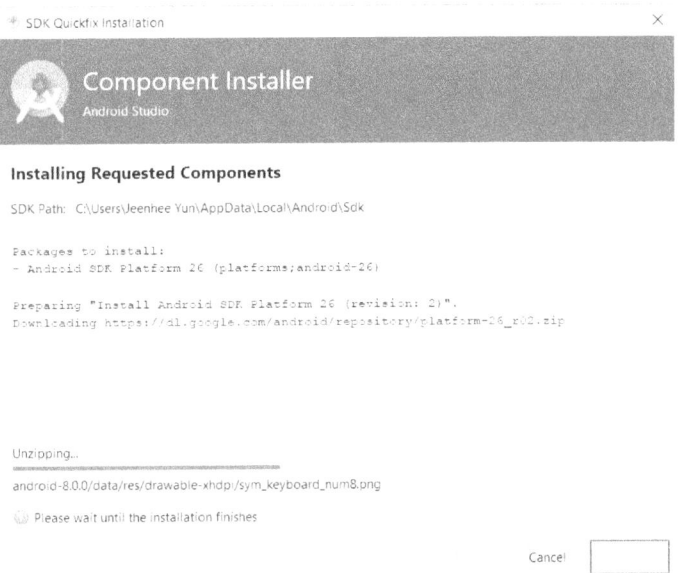

If the example is run on the phone, it is successful. Now you can play your own games anywhere, and you can enjoy with your friends.

[Exercise] Install old source project to smart phone
1. Open one of old source projects. (Number up & down game, Even & Odd game, Gugu Game)

2. Connect Phone and PC by using USB cable. And install source project to phone.

- Good job. Thank you -

Java Coing with Android programming series

1. Java Language Beginner - 1

[Development Environment & Variable & Conditional sentence (if else, switch case)]

2. Java Language Beginner - 2

[Function & Repeat command (for, while, do while) & Array]

3. Android API Beginner - 1

[Basic widget(UI control) & Android application development beginner 1]

4. Android API Beginner - 2

[Screen layout & Android application development beginner 2]

5. Android API Beginner - 3

[Basic API & Android application development beginner 3]

```
Author : Dennis (Donggeun Jung)
Email : topsan72@gmail.com
   topofsan@naver.com
```

www.ingramcontent.com/pod-product-compliance
Lightning Source LLC
Chambersburg PA
CBHW080943240526
45469CB00019B/2927